Chronicles of Truth

by

Jen Ward

Copyright © 2017 Jen Ward

All rights reserved. No part of this book may be reproduced, stored in a retrieval system, or transmitted in any form by any means, whether electronic, mechanical, photocopying, recording, or otherwise, without written permission of the author.

Uploaded through CreateSpace November 2017

ISBN-10: 0-9994954-1-0
ISBN-13: 978-0-9994954-1-4

JEN WARD

CONTENTS

	Introduction	1
1	World Peace on the Other Side of the Veil	3
2	How to Transcend	8
3	Dismantle Psychic Policing	13
4	How to Remove Yourself from Linear Existence	22
5	Learning How to Access Truth	27
6	Spiritual Opportunity	34
7	Power Versus Purpose	38
8	Deductive Reasoning	41
9	Abolishing Racism	45
10	From Congress to Integrity	54
11	What Is Being Infused back into Humanity?	64
12	Fossil Fuel	67
13	Many Hands	73
14	Freeing the World of a Dark Force	76
15	Lowest Common Denominator	86
16	Cleaning the Slate of All Old Engrams	92
17	Dealing with Trolls in Life	105

18	Have You Been Feeling the Upgrades?	108
19	Eliminate Dark Money	110
20	Moving from Linear to Exponential	119
21	Free Humanity of All Drugs, Opioids and Addictions	126
22	What Aware Souls Do	137
23	The Quickest Route to Transcendence	143
24	Dissipating More Psychic Streams of Energy	150
25	Exodus and the Lymphatic System	157
26	Free Yourself of Taking That Last Breath	161
27	The Heart Chakra of the Universe	165
28	Your Validation	172
29	How We Awaken	175
30	If You Value Trees, Or How to Be a World Savior	182
31	Removing Shackles Upon Truth	187
32	How Do I Tell?	195
33	Forgo the Wielding of Power	199
34	The Saving Grace of Humanity	205
35	A Desecration to the Advancement of Soul	211
36	Your Gift to the World	216
37	Prevent a Manufactured War	225

38	Regaining Spiritual Perspective	235
39	Taking Classes in the Dream State	244

About the Author	248
Other Books by Jen Ward	251

INTRODUCTION

Truth and love resonate at similar frequencies. The reason there is not more love in the world is because there is little truth. Slanting truth is as ridiculous as slanting love. But slanting truth has been a tool for control for as long as we have been in existence. Unfortunately, truth has been so diluted and distorted by different factions that people have lost the art of tapping into direct knowing for themselves. They are at the mercy of the controlling beliefs of those in power.

Truth is like a cleansing agent for the stagnant minutia that collects on our psyche and renders us inoperable as energy beings. Truth sears away the layers of inertia to reveal to ourselves glimmers of our empowerment.

This book is intended to validate the readers by sharing truths with them to the depth they will not read in any other modern pages. Many people don't realize that they are afraid of truth. Because for all of history, truth has been power. Individuals are now afraid of abusing power. The truths in this book are a means to coax the reader out of their inhibitions and accept the fact that they can indeed handle the truth. Not only can they handle the truth, but they can discover how to mine truth in the depth of their own beingness.

1: WORLD PEACE ON THE OTHER SIDE OF THE VEIL

Send your love through the world and flush away all that is not in accord with the most pure expression of you, which is love. Each individual has the potential to heal, uplift, teach and empower the whole world if they merely realize their own capabilities. You all have the heart and ability to do so. All you need is the resolve.

Once in a while, a soul will stumble into its greatness through insurmountable need or circumstance. Just as the Gandhi's, the Martin Luther King Jr.'s and the Mother Teresa's did. The way and means to greatness are different to all but are also accessible to all. The rise in consciousness that we collectively are experiencing is the realization that we all are in a position to empower the world in manifesting Universal Peace. That is why the majority of us are seeing through the veil of manipulation of power. We are no longer moved into a knee-jerk response of fear and hate. It is our time to take that awareness to the next level and exude and expound our love into all life. The shackles to our empowerment are off.

It comes through the way of your heart, your passion, that thing in your life that breaks you open to great empathy and compassion. It's that memory of being on the receiving end of injustice. Do what you can to serve kindness and the way will be opened for you to step through to your greatness. You will then lead the multitudes to theirs. Imagine a world where all do just this and there will be that elusive world peace that we all, in our heart of hearts, still hold a place for.

I woke up very tired this morning. Maybe some of you have as well. In this world, there feels a bit of an emptiness and a lack of motivation. It may feel like a negative thing. But here is a more exponential explanation. Last night, on the other side of the veil, there were different kinds of parties going on. It was similar to everyone having great New Year's parties. But these parties were celebrating world peace.

I had visited a few of them. There was one that was all about dancing. I was listening to my cousin who is very passionate about sharing his love of dance with the world. We were at a very lively dance party and everyone was having the time of their life. There were also other parties I was attending. Time is not linear on the other side of the veil. So I was at many celebrations at once.

There was one for light workers on earth. They were all celebrating under a starry sky. It was an incredible, joyful event. There was even one event that was more of a family picnic celebration. One had a small town feel that exuded the feeling of everyone in a small close knit community embracing the festivities.

Maybe many of you have woken up tired. Maybe you converted it into a negative feeling. It is only because the atoms of our physical make-up have been conditioned to convert experiences they are not used to processing, into negative feelings. It may have the feel of being let down after a major accomplishment like graduation. It is merely a spaciousness that is created in our consciousness that needs to be allowed to exist without being filled with a negative response. This is a new discipline for many of us who have studied towards spiritual mastership and have disciplined ourselves to do. We can now do this easily with a little awareness. We are not swimming upstream in such negative currents anymore. We are free to wade in our expansiveness.

As you make space for this uncomfortable feeling within yourself, without trying to quantify it, you are holding space for Universal Peace. Let all the hate and power mongers use up their last wad of control. It is alright. They need to learn the lessons very quickly that we have had lifetimes to collect and process. Be grateful that they are being used as the catalysts for society to draw out the last dregs of power and extract them from the fabrics of humanity. There is no need to counter them. There is no need to bottle feed them awareness. They are getting it through osmosis.

It is better to just know in your place of nudges and gut feelings that what I am explaining here is higher truth. That the illusion of this world is breaking away to Universal Peace and Freedom. The less energy we waste on trying to fight the negative currents that are on display right now, the more we withdraw our energy from perpetuating them.

Think of the display of power mongering we are all blatantly watching as a spectacular light show for us all to witness. To react to them is no more effective than trying to punch a ghost. They are merely the old consciousness of negativity being burned off the new state of a new earth. It's no different from the alcohol being burned off a fine sherry that is used for cooking. Just the hint of our struggles is the seasoning of gratitude for a new dawn.

Universal Peace is coming. You don't have to try to figure out how. That would be like trying to figure out how to personally connect with people all over the planet before the Internet and social media were established. How something manifests is that it is experienced on the more subtle realms first. This allows it to disseminate into the coarser vibration of the physical realms. That is why so many inventions for the world start out in the finer vibration of the mental realm. People then see them manifested on the astral realms in their dreams. They then use their ingenuity, passion and determination to bring them down into the physical realm. They then become the fabric of our Universal experience.

Maybe you remember that celebration on the astral plane that I am referring to. Maybe it will ease your angst in trying to understand current events. We have all been waiting to experience this incarnation when humanity ascends. Please enjoy the process. We all have earned it. Please feel my love and the connection with the multitudes that love. Everything else will soon be inconsequential as we awaken to the wonder of exponential joy, love, wondrous abundance, freedom and peace. Holding space for such things can do wonders.

I love you all. Thank you for being present and aware.

2: HOW TO TRANSCEND

Cut the Drama. The emotions are very low on the survival scale. Being reactionary is being in primal mode. So to be dramatic is to marry two low level vibrations. Existing in them is a means to ensure that you will stay at a primal level of existence. You cannot connect to truth and your deeper self if you are in reactionary mode. Even the crudest animals don't do this. Being dramatic is a very ignorant way to entertain yourself and ensure attention. It is pulling humanity down.

Refrain from all derogatory verbiage and behavior. This includes about yourself. The humility that has been ingrained in humanity is a form of having people inflict imprisonment on themselves. Humility is merely having the same sense of value for others that you have for yourself. There is no need to lower the bar on all of humanity by seeing yourself or others as unworthy. Those who control others do not do this. So all individuals need to take this "edge" away from power mongers by reseeding humanity. We do this when we see everyone with great value and worth.

Speak clear truth. Insults are not truth. Truth has a neutral charge, not a negative one. Truth is not opinions or anything that is heard in the media. Truth comes from a depth that strikes the censors of the gut and heart. Listening to lies is not being polite. It is behaving untruthfully. If the neutrality of truth hurts, then it is layers of illusion being ripped off of someone who identified with the illusion. These layers need to go, from ourselves and from all others. It doesn't mean it is our job to rip layers off. It just means we shouldn't cringe from the task when we are led to speak truth by our higher self. Compassion and neutrality together are great partnerships in rendering truth.

Stop defending a cause. All causes and ideologies are of the mind nature. There is a more expansive consciousness beyond them. Defending any cause or ideology is stating to the Universe and all others that you are afraid to transcend. Fear is the opposite of love.

Please stop defending God. God is the Source of all in its true essence. God does not need defending. God does not need the ego stroked. God has no ego. Man has been duped into worshiping a manmade concept. Anything that limits, diminishes, judges and impinges the freedom of individuals in any way is not mandated by God, but is the opposite. All of this worship of God in an unloving way towards others is following false prophets. ALL OF IT. It keeps humanity in victim mode. It is a distraction from seeing your own empowerment.

Delighting in debate, opinions and other mind games is only indulging and entertaining the ego. Nobody has learned truth by talking. Talking is a means of projecting your vibration out to others to proclaim you exist. It is fear based. The louder someone is, the more afraid they are in energy. Think about the people who are playing their music really loud in the car. At the core, they are not doing it to be irritating. They are doing it because they are terrified. In energy, they are doing it to keep predators away. It is easier to have compassion for them when you can realize this. In the same way, those who lecture others and tell them what to do are terrified in energy of how little they know.

Stop competing with others. Stop "one-upping" others. This means there is no hierarchy, comparisons, or trying to emulate others. Everyone is a starburst. Their uniqueness is in their unpredictable emanations. This is their display against the backdrop of conformity. If you try to align two starbursts, you hinder both of their patterns of emanation. You drop them both out of the sky.

Root for the other gal. Life isn't about bettering others. Life is about all of us being the best. This is how we raise the bar on humanity. Those inspiring images of one runner carrying the other runner over the finish line are great analogies of how to live. Let's carry each other over the finish line in all the ways that we can. Allowing ourselves to be carried over the finish line when relevant is important too.

Practicing random kindness is the mainstay of a loving existence. That is why being kind feels so good; it is contributing to raising the bar on humanity.

Stop converting all forms of abundance to the monetary system. It is old currency. Doing something that you don't love or that does not make you happy or taxes your body is a form of selling your soul for money. Your energy system runs and thrives on joy, truth and love. If you do not love what you do, and it does not bring you joy, then you are not being truthful to yourself. An energy system that does what it loves perpetually feeds itself. One that doesn't may have monetary wealth but taxes humanity in a different way. The rich think those who don't generate great wealth are a tax on society. But those who live only to generate more wealth at the cost of a clean and safe environment are taxing all of humanity.

Bring creativity, imagination, individual expression and enthusiasm back to life. These were all but stripped out of humanity by the power mongers who tried to enslave us all to a linear existence. But they were not merely attempting to enslave us on earth. They were attempting to dry up our afterlife as well. Our afterlife consists of the God stuff we generate in this life. A renaissance of creativity and expression is needed. Not only to generate goodness on earth but to reseed the heavens. This is the great necessity of having children: to regenerate the imagination of us all. Programming them extra early with stringent schedules and computers is robbing all of humanity of childlike wonder as a resource to regenerate our own creative expression.

This is a short list. If people can digest some of these truths and emanate them out into humanity as a mainstay, we will well be on our way to getting back on course to worldwide peace.

3: DISMANTLE PSYCHIC POLICING

Morality is an inside job. The only one who can dictate integrity is our own moral compass. It is a connection with our own truth. Everything I write and share is dictated to me in energy and I transcribe it into words. I have become very proficient at listening to my Guides. It has kept me alive and has served me well. My Guides are my friends and equals. I do not sit at their feet.

All my posts are designed to free individuals from the grip of mass control. I have been writing and sharing daily techniques, poems, insights, taps, inspirational quotes and observations for the last nine years. It is all about gifting the world with higher awareness. I am a very gifted healer as well. Truth and love resonate at similar frequencies, so if there is more truth in the world, there is more love.

Many people have told me to stop sharing so much because it ruins my business. It meets people's needs without them needing a session with me. Good. I have watched the freedom and awareness that is blooming in the world and I sincerely know that I have initiated that with my work. I did not come here merely to provide food for my table. I have come here to empower all individuals to make space in this world for Universal Peace.

It is interesting though, that people who have benefitted from my work still feel the right to police what I do. They compare themselves to me, lecture me, brag about their abilities and try to hold me to their understanding of morality based on a knee-jerk reaction. They have revealed the reason so many people are afraid to speak their truth. It is because of psychic policing. The "mean girl" mentality does not just show up in high school. It may be subtle, but it even shows up in spiritual circles.

Just yesterday, I got distracted from my work a few times by this psychic policing. I was writing about current events. I wrote about political issues because they are learning tools for those awakening to the subtle ways of power. In teaching spiritual law, there is no better way to help individuals take back their empowerment than by addressing blatantly obvious injustices that we are all watching play out.

Politics is where individual energy has been collected. It used to be as subtle as a sundry tax, but now it is depleting the life force of individuals who do not realize how to protect themselves. I show everyone how to do that. It is as simple as refusing to pay a tax. If everyone refused to pay taxes all at once, the government would collapse. When people refuse to give their energy to power groups, they will be dismantled as well.

I am teaching people to energetically refuse to give their energy to groups that are fleecing their life force. It is working. That is why all these power mongers and their web of connections are more recognizable. As individuals withdraw their energy from power groups, they lose the ability to dominate and bulldoze over individual souls. People are now exercising this by showing up and protesting. That is evidence of a shift. These groups love it when people feel helpless or beholden to them. That is how they thrive. That is what gives them their magnetic shine.

In energy, diminishing these groups is not done simply by protesting but by withdrawing your energy of support or allegiance to these groups. That is why patriotism is ruthlessly mandated. Patriotism is a means of energetically taxing the individuals. It just is. I can love and have gratitude for all the gifts of existing in America, but if I don't have patriotism, I am not adding to the coffers. It is as important as keeping the power grids working. That is why the psychic police are ruthless about demanding patriotism.

Very aware souls know this principle innately and have come to not feeling patriotism anymore. They have sensed the dynamic of it taxing their energy. Ethical leaders do not require demonstrative admiration. They understand it is a mandate that is used to feed power. It doesn't feed anything loving. It feeds power. That is how one can gauge their concept of God. If it needs stroking, it is not God but power. The psychic police set up the concept of worshiping God as a means to extract energy from the loyal.

Notice the leaders who demand that individuals tout loyalty to country. They are the same ones who are using individual energy for ill gain. In fact, some of us can see someone demanding patriotism as a sign that they are operating from a more judgmental, energetically coarse platform. Those who don't demand such demonstrative displays are less energetically taxing individuals. It is good not to be energetically taxed. Then you are free to use all your energy towards a more noble intention of true honoring of Source through outflowing to others from Source within.

These people who scan our words and actions for infractions are psychic police. Their job is to keep fringe elements from wandering out of group dynamics and breaking the psychic force field that is used as a fence to contain them. In a way, they police a psychic wall. The wall is a very spiritual analogy of wanting to contain people in mass control. Labels are another means of containing. That is why I consider the term "light worker" an oxymoron. The label itself is a containment of spiritual individuals. A true light worker doesn't resonate so easily with labels.

These psychic police maintain any kind of group by shaming the individuals and calling them out if they wander away from the mandated belief. They are ruthlessly protecting an energetic containment of some kind. We see this happening in religions, politics, families and even in social groups. It has become systemic bullying and the only means to really keep people "in" at this point. Those awakening have lost their fear of what lies beyond the border. They know it is freedom.

Yesterday, I was confronted by a few of these psychic police over what I said. I got lectured that my comments were unkind (they were not), and people who have read my page for years and must realize my pure intention were now calling me out for what I posted. Now, I realize that some people who read my page are not here to benefit themselves but are acting as psychic police for spiritual principles. They think they have well intentions but they are patrolling the wall for infractions. As soon as I say something that is lessening their belief of what they have been told is spirituality, they are ready to admonish.

This has actually put a glass ceiling on spiritual awakening because some of the most spiritually savvy people I know have been moonlighting as psychic police. But since I work from a vantage point that others are not at, I can see what others cannot see.

It is interesting how so many people like to declare that we are at the same level especially when they are defying spiritual law. They are not at my vantage point, or else they would not need to make a point we are equals. They are trying to use my vibration to raise their own, but they are really trying to pull me down. I usually do not address this unless they are harming others. Psychic police are harming others. People who try to discredit truth need to be seen.

Most people don't know truth. They only know opinion. Opinion is not truth. I post truth. It resonates with a caliber of integrity. People need to feel this vibration and know how to resonate with it themselves. Psychic police do not want people to be so free. They may want to be more special than others in order to have an edge. This is what male energy does. They attempt to discredit me to maintain their special edge. In energy, it is a full-on assault. In words, it may seem harmless. But make no mistake; those subtle feelings of being assaulted are real.

Now that I have pointed it out, people reading this are having lights of recognition go off. They will be able to recognize who has been doing this to them. It has all been done for power, control and to maintain a linear reality. But we are no longer contained in a linear timeline. We are exponential beings and, as such, we are empowered to maintain our own moral compass in all ways and in all matters of concern. This is spiritual freedom.

Anyone who psychically polices you is interfering with your spiritual freedom. In lower vibrations, laws do this. Many of us see the problem with dictating personal choice as far as morality. Mandating laws that infringe on personal freedom is a very crude form of psychic policing. But psychic policing scans the polarity of very rudimentary choices to very refined choices like in how to conduct yourself as a spiritual being.

Some of the rules of spiritual psychic policing are:

- don't help anyone because they need to have the experience to strengthen themselves;
- don't heal anyone or you will take on their karma;
- people need to fight it out, this is a warring universe;
- you need to get out of the body to be spiritual;
- you need to gain perfection;
- you need to give your adoration to someone outside of yourself for protection;
- you need to ask permission before you heal someone.

All of these maintain the walls around spirituality so that people don't break out into their empowerment.

Of course it is okay to help others. Humanity has been shackled by power. If you saw an abused dog chained up, wouldn't you help it? Even if it were biting at you?

You tap into truth from within. You don't need to put a man's face on it so the chambers open up. Of course there will be things that seem scary. Fear is a gauge that you are getting closer to breaking through a wall and that you need to apply more love.

There is even the belief that truth must not be shared openly or it will be used to harm others. At this point, truth needs to be in the hands of everyone to level the playing field because the only ones who have been accessing such principles are those who have been leveraging them against humanity. That is the reason I have been put in this position to defy all psychic policing and share all I can with those who are awakening. It is a necessary step in the awakening of humanity.

By the way, there are people who are at my vantage point, but they are never the ones who need to declare it. Either they are too busy assisting humanity in their own way or they don't even realize their own depth because they have been feigning off an onslaught of psychic attacks. But here is to us helping them. It may well be you.

Please do these taps. Now that we can see psychic

policing, it can no longer have such a hold over humanity. Let's remove its effectiveness.

(Say each statement three times while tapping on your head and say it a fourth time while tapping on your chest.)

"I declare myself a surrogate for humanity in doing these taps; in all moments."

"I dismantle the practice of psychic policing; in all moments."

"I release being a contributor of psychic policing; in all moments."

"I withdraw all my energy from psychic policing; in all moments."

"I strip all layers of illusion and authority away from all psychic policing; in all moments."

"I disarm all agents of psychic policing; in all moments."

"I collapse and dissolve all limitations or walls maintained by psychic policing; in all moments."

"I nullify all contracts with psychic policing; in all moments."

"I shift my paradigm from psychic policing to spiritual freedom; in all moments."

"I transcend psychic policing; in all moments."

4: HOW TO REMOVE YOURSELF FROM LINEAR EXISTENCE

Life is like a netting of illusion. Thinking about the past or worrying about the future pulls the drawstring of the netting around you more. It is an energetic way of ensuring yourself you will never lose the security of your netting.

Immersing yourself in the moment is a way of loosening the drawstring on the netting and allowing a big enough opening to remove yourself. If you practice this enough, it allows the netting to fall away.

This is what meditation was supposed to achieve for people. But many people merely use the practice as a means to tolerate the netting. The fabric of the netting is made up of the same mind energy that is used in meditation. It is difficult to differentiate the resolve from the thing that contains us.

There are many ways to remove yourself from linear existence and expound yourself into an exponential reality.

Do things you love. Anything that gets you lost in the moment is actually pulling you out of time and space. Love itself melts away the netting and allows all things to be possible. We have been led to deduce love as a corny concept because of its concentrated power to free us as individuals and all of humanity as well. All individuals have the capability of changing the world with their love if only they have the capacity and capability to do so. A great technique is to consciously practice loving all the people, species and atoms in the world. It is easier to do if you imagine the world as smaller as a means to wrap your head and heart around it.

Visualizations and using the imagination are dynamic means of stepping out of the netting. If done consistently, one can be the commander of the netting instead of trapped in it. This is what creative geniuses do. The possibilities are available to all.

Don't nail down your life in time. Every time you make an appointment, you are nailing yourself into time and space. It is necessary to make some appointments to function in this linear world, but the more you can leave your calendar open, the more free you will be.

Don't fill your intentions with empty promises. If you say you are going to do something, ensure that you do it. When you don't, you split your energy into two paths: the you that walks around and the intention you set out. The more you send out false intentions, the more you dilute your effectiveness in life. You will end up showing up merely as a projection screen image in life and not really be immersed in it. Your energy will literally have no integrity. Integrity is having your intentions and you always on the same page. It is a dynamic, effective person who does this.

Stop talking and thinking about the past. Stop talking and worrying about the future. Thoughts are like little barbs that hook us into the netting of illusion. They are what tangle us up instead of allowing us freedom in our own beingness. Feelings are clipping us in as well. The more you can catch yourself being in the past or future, the more you can bring yourself into the present. The present is the portal to expound.

Question everything you have been told to believe. Most of our conditioning has been to keep us immersed in a linear form of slavery. Pay attention to how much you have been conditioned to move along in life like it is a conveyor belt: birth to death, nine to five, season to season. When you follow the mandates of conditioning, you are on autopilot and not free to expound. This is why creative types seem so non-committal. They are.

Stop thinking of life and death with such division. Heaven is not a place. It is a state of consciousness. It is a vibration that overlays this one yet at a more subtle frequency. When someone dies, they merely drop the course vibration of this world and then exist at the finer frequency. They are still themselves as much as ever and are so much closer than we fathom. They are right outside that netting of illusion of a linear reality. This netting is what prevents us from connecting with them.

Be grateful. Gratitude is a physiological process of opening your chakras to receive more energy. They open like an aperture of a camera. It isn't emotions that open them. It is the greater flux of energy that gives us the warm feeling when grateful. It is a physiological process. We use gratitude as a shortcut to do this. But if someone has a hard time mocking up gratitude, perhaps they will have better luck merely setting the intention to consciously open up the chakras. This will bypass the need to emote gratitude.

Talk less. Talking is filled with all these barbs that keep us immersed in the netting. I personally exist without the netting on as much as possible. When I listen to others, it is a means of being wrapped in the netting. When you talk about problems, you are giving the coordinates of them in time and space and sending others to that misery. It is pretty low on the survival scale to do this. It is how we have been trained to keep each other trapped.

Even light workers are limited by linear existence. When you visualize energy coming in the top of your head and out your feet, this is a linear understanding of energy. Energy is pouring into you on all sides and at all angles at all times. You are not a solid body but an emanating starburst of energy. The more you see yourself sending out and receiving love and beautiful intentions in every direction, the more you will grasp a higher concept of yourself.

Every time you label yourself, you are nailing yourself in time and space. At one time, we all perceived in energy. It is a subtler but more accurate awareness. Not perceiving in energy is a form of being blind. Labels are a way for those who are blind to feel around in the dark for what they are looking for. That is why the more unaware someone is, the more there is a need for labels. The unaware depend on labels to find their way around. Labels are also a way that groups keep us in the sheep mentality. They use labels to keep us blind and so easier to control. When a group is hell-bent on using a label, realize that they are really hell-bent on control.

When you breathe, you are not merely inhaling and exhaling. You are communing with all of life. You are sending out from your energy field, atoms of life imprinted with your unique vantage point. You are sharing all that you are with the Universe. In return, you accept in all the information it has to give you which is imprinted in the atoms of air you take in. In this exchange, we are exchanging the information and vantage point of all beings. There is much wisdom in our breath. We would benefit from being consciously aware of that as a means of better digesting the information we receive. It is little different from conscious eating.

5: LEARNING HOW TO ACCESS TRUTH

I will be interviewed during a call-in event tonight answering questions about the first healing retreat that I will be facilitating. It will mark a shift in world consciousness. It is epic for anyone who sees that. That is why so much in current events is in flux right now. It is the polar opposite to balance what is transpiring this weekend at the first retreat.

Why is this event different from any other self-help event? Because I will be teaching all the participants how to tap into truth for themselves so that the art of accessing truth is never again lost to the planet. Truth came pretty close to waning out of existence. Those who pay attention to subtle things may have been getting a sense of this. Many were feeling all was lost. With this retreat, hope is regained. Truth, integrity and even peace will spill out through the streets.

Unless truth is updated regularly, it is no longer truth but stagnant energy. It becomes rhetoric, opinion or even conjecture. Truth is like a perpetual well that springs from an infinite source within. It is always being updated. We witness how quickly current events change and how often technology is updated. So why isn't every day truth ever questioned, and why is our connection to truth so muddled? We exist in an outmoded reality. It has been discouraging at best.

We see the evidence of lack of truth playing out in current events. Truth has become as random and as entrenched as the agenda it is holding up. People confuse facts for truth and many don't realize the difference. Facts are a set of circumstances based on a linear vantage point. Truth is universal. Life stopped being a daily harvesting of creativity and adventure the day male energy withheld truth from the masses for their own good and sold it to them in secret sects.

We have been told that the dark ages are over. But they never ended. Not as long as individuals are fed so many conditions and criteria for truth. There should be no restrictions put on what is accessed. Truth, like abundance and goodwill, should be flooding the streets.

New truths are perpetually pouring through me all the time. They should be pouring through everyone. There should be uplifting art, new inventions, great insights, celestial music, enthusiasm and even goodwill flooding the streets and social media. There should be a renaissance of creativity and a plethora of innovations to sustain the organic resources of humanity. But they have all been squelched by male energy to drive individuals to supporting different agendas. It is great that we are seeing how systemic this is in the world. It is a literal wake up call to humanity to stop listening to outside sources on anything regarding great truth. Accessing truth is an inner and personal undertaking. The skills to do so have been all but lost. That is why my retreats are different.

In any usual event prior, there is a charismatic figurehead donning out great truths to the supporters from a superior position. I have never considered myself charismatic nor am I someone who people have naturally listened to. As a matter of fact, I have been overlooked more than a needle in a haystack and have been just as invisible. In some ways, I have seemed to stick in one's skin like a needle and really irritate them with no intention of doing so. I have come to realize that even the presence of truth in a silent form is an irritant to an agenda. So many of us have been conditioned to have a literal aversion to truth as if it were a high starched collar one is forced to wear. But no. Accessing truth is as joyous and adventurous as living a perpetual epiphany in a world of a multi-dimensional jigsaw puzzle.

So some of the things that will be addressed during the retreat are things never really posed in a group setting:

- Why all groups are like energetic Ponzi schemes and deter individuality; this truth is being revealed in some people's natural aversion to groups.

- Why it is as limiting for someone to be put on a pedestal as it is to put someone else on one; freeing yourself from caring what people think or even if they like you.

- How to strip off the layers of conditioning that prevent someone from accessing truth.

- How to know yourself so you can know your purpose.

- Eliminate old engrams and Akashic records that are no longer necessary in the new dimension.

- How to recognize truth using your own inner compass.

- Learn all the outmoded schools of thought that were limiting the upliftment of all humanity. (For example, why it is impossible to take on someone's karma or how not to take on others' karma?)

- Understand the limitations of the linear conditions that we all have been living within.

- How to burst into an exponential existence.

- How to awaken your subtle senses and learn to perceive in energy.

- The physiology of faith healing: Using subtle senses to perceive stagnant energy and using an intention to clear it. Going from faith to knowing.

- Learn how the world got skewed from balance by adhering to a male slanted narrative.

- The history of the bastardization of female energy and how humanity is balancing that out in present time.

- How to self-heal, nurture, guide, teach, affirm, love and reclaim abundance.

- New hope for World Peace and how it looks nothing like a static condition.

- How the chains to time and space and even monetary abundance are being freed from humanity.

- How important it is to pour truth out into the masses instead of sitting on it with the promise of making a buck.

- The difference between a male driven society of competition and a female empowered humanity of sisterhood (regardless of genital or sexual orientation).

- The beauty and necessity of diversity.

- How vital the caliber and vibration of everything you say and even think is to maintain the vibration of the fifth dimension.

- Each attendee will be given access to all the truth, love, energy and understanding that I am able to download into them (If two smart phones can share information, why can't two living organisms?)

In short, I will give everyone everything that I have of truth, love and a means to awaken so that they can take it with them and pour it out into the streets and to their loved ones. The days of doling it out in increments are gone. All of humanity will have access to all that is needed to reawaken systemic truth, integrity, kindness, enthusiasm, purpose, health and abundance. Mark your outmoded calendar because it starts here.

Truth and love vibrate at a similar frequency. If you want there to be more love in the world, there needs to be the fertile ground of truth for it to be maintained. This is one of the many imbalances that will be addressed at the weekend retreat. I have been groomed many lifetimes to be strong enough in a female body to assist all others to their own empowerment. It is my purpose to fulfill. May you know and embrace yours as readily.

We are all intrinsically in tune with each other, so the whole planet will be gaining awareness with this retreat. It may just be more of a treasure for those who recognize the opportunity and take the initiative to come.

6: SPIRITUAL OPPORTUNITY

Some events only seem special in hindsight. Nobody could have predicted the ramifications of Woodstock. What about making salt with Gandhi? Or the Million Man March?

When I was locked up, starved and tortured, even though I was a nobody, I had the sense that some force was trying to prevent me from carrying on my mission. It was a mission that had not yet revealed itself to me. But I had an innate sense that if I survived, I would be renowned in a positive way that would uplift humanity.

That was over nine years ago. I had returned to society believing I was a retarded boy. I had no sense of the many books I would write all chock full of tools and techniques to help the individual to be empowered. I now have ten. I had no idea of the protocol of tapping I would present to the world that would teach everyone to remove the chains of their own issues. I could not possibly realize how desperately my assistance is needed right now.

When I was younger, I was told by my Spirit Guides that I was the reincarnation of Madame Blavatsky. But I was a nobody, and it was still silly back then to believe in such things. It wasn't until a few short years ago that I jokingly held her book up to my own photograph and the person with me dropped his jaw. The likeness was uncanny. Since then, I have been told my writing is similar to hers and my persona may be similar to hers as well. It is something that people who studied her enjoy experiencing in me. We are both no-nonsense in similar ways.

The dreams that kept me alive during my captivity were of many people waiting for an event to begin in a very nice hotel. Those dreams were foreshadowing the event that I facilitated the next weekend in Rochester, NY. Those dreams kept me alive. My Guides wanted me to survive at all costs. Everything that I write and teach is ordained by Ancient Beings who have been guiding my course from invisible realms.

When I was on the property where I was imprisoned, I knew, if I survived, that I would be assisting humanity in an incredible way. Many times, the choice was mine whether I would live or die. With the difficulties of this life, perhaps not. But I do know that I have the resiliency, fortitude and endurance to assist all souls in recognizing themselves as omniscient beings. It is a miracle that I have gotten to the point to be able to present truth and an upgrade to healing practices to those who recognize the opportunity.

I can read the Akashic records as easily as people can scroll the Internet. I see many people very disappointed that they didn't take this time to meet me and personally learn from me when they still had the chance. There is still time. You are all invited to attend and receive a huge upgrade to your own awakening. Learn about the retreats at www.jenuinehealing.com.

People ask if there will be another retreat because the timing is inconvenient. I am amused because I see the Akashic records of all that we have endured to get to this point of awakening that this event marks. In the subtle realms, there is a celebration that humanity has arrived at this pinnacle. I am not sure of future events. I know this is the one that matters.

In Madame Blavatsky's original edition of *Isis Unveiled*, she spoke of Rochester, New York as a great portal for higher energies to flood into the physical world. She was speaking of her work in a future generation. The work I am doing now. The floodgates will be opened up at the retreat I am facilitating this upcoming weekend. As a coincidence, or as a breadcrumb to lead a trail to her future work, Madame Blavatsky's first book was published in Rochester, NY. The bookstore is called Small World Books. It is still operational.

When I visited there a few months ago, a very seasoned,

disinterested caretaker jumped out of his seat to shake my hand. It was a timeless exchange as if he had been keeping the bookstore open all these lifetimes to welcome me back. I look forward to meeting a lot of old friends still in this lifetime.

Many people who come to me have a respect for Madame Blavatsky. They say they were researching something about her and came across information about me.

I would like to think that I am taking up the work that I did in that lifetime. It is as if that lifetime was about collecting and assimilating all the truth available, and this life is about simplifying it so it is easily assimilated by others.

7: POWER VS. PURPOSE

Dear Democrats and Republicans,

Let's face it. This system is not working. Both sides have their pet agendas and you are splitting the country apart with worshiping them instead of working for the people. Their ploys have become transparent to us. We no longer are falling victim to their lies, rhetoric, passionate pleas or outrage.

The power players can't even stand their own bullshit anymore. I wonder if selling out their integrity will affect them for lifetimes to come. What must it feel like to be them? How uncomfortable they must feel in their skin. Do they even feel any more? Or, have they morphed into the non-feeling drones that their actions suggest?

We get it. One side is anti abortion, pro gun and use God and country to hold their constituents into an emotional state of paralysis and ignorance. The problem is that hypocrisy is pretty transparent. The way they advocate for war, deportation and big business at the expense of individuals is obvious. They are against any assistance to those who aren't born with a clear pathway to success and show little compassion for the disadvantaged. The only demographic they are willing to go to bat for is the fetus and the affluent white. It is THEN and only then that their moral code kicks in.

The other side is more subtle in their deceit. They really seem to care. But some in the party use the downtrodden like a human shield of morality to push their own agenda. You may be corrupted by power and wealth as well but are just more savvy at hiding your agendas.

So now, there is the dividing line. It is no longer the "them versus us" between political parties or any offshoot of a political party. The politician that gains favor is the one who breaks lines with the agenda and puts his reputation and career on the line for what is right and just. It is appalling to most of the world that so many are falling in line with the lowest bar ever set for the office of presidency. Shame on all of you. The new political defining line is between self-serving and serving out of purpose.

Humanity will survive this current affront on justice and truth, but will the individuals involved? Will current events cloud and the present fleeting reign of power be what defines certain individuals in history? Or, will some show up as heroes in some way by defying the balm that tries to rest upon our great land? Is this how our forefathers' dreams die--tucked away in someone's vest pocket? Or, will individuals emerge with an integrity and strength that they have not exercised since youth?

We the people are watching. We are watching all individuals and players and what moves motivates them. Current events we are experience in this historic period is deserving of our contempt. It is those who have served this great nation half of their life who are under scrutiny. Have they done so with integrity and intention. Or have they used their position as a cushy place to wield their power and grab a paycheck. A worm can only do what a worm does. But those who allow corruption to worm its way into the highest political offices and allow it to go unchecked are a problem. Shame on all of those who have brought this plague to the people. May they all be visited by an epiphany to do what they need to do and fix this.

8: DEDUCTIVE REASONING

Most of us are seeing the hypocrisy play out in the media. We are seeing the slanted point of view, the manipulation, the power plays and burying of truth. We are even seeing the bias and obtuse reasoning in regard to electing our highest officials. Most of us realize that what we are seeing is an infomercial for a particular agenda of someone with a pretty thick wallet. We are all witnessing this.

So when did this exploitation and blatant lying to people start? A year ago? Twenty? Fifty? Or always? It has *always been occurring*. This is what people don't understand. Everything they know and think is absolute truth has been formulated by someone with an agenda: our morals, our understanding of life, our interaction with others and even our relationship with God.

We look at things other cultures believe in and realize that they are naïve. They are being manipulated or are being blatantly lied to. Worshipping cows, seventy-two virgins, only one life. They are all serving a purpose in formulating a particular belief and keeping the populace confined to a particular agenda. Even the lie that America is as pure as the driven snow and is superior and entitled in its treatment of other cultures is a form of cultivated bias. I love America; I am grateful to live here, but it is biased.

We are all outgrowing being manipulated from without. It has created a systemic, worldwide, enslaved mentality. The only way to rectify this and free humanity is for everyone to start thinking for themselves and questioning everything that they have ever been told and just assumed. Develop an inner compass to gauge truth, and look at everything that you are presented with like a five year old child that is just being told something for the very first time.

I have learned to do this. It caused a great depression in me in the early eighties when I was disillusioned with Reagan being president. I innately realized that he was basically hired as a figurehead and was acting through his whole presidency. His whole policy of giving to the rich and allowing it to trickle down to the rest didn't quite work that way.

It has caused the incredible slant in wealth that we all see today. I knew it would. I had to live with that awareness while the world blissfully sung his praises. But he was a paid actor playing a part. He was reading the scripts given to him. You can see the black magicians wielding their illusion when you hear otherwise.

It is time for everyone to wake up from a stupor. Everything I share is poking holes in a curtain of illusion that has been our mainstay. People don't like to be woken up. But it is no longer a pleasant dream but a nightmare. We must wake up and gain our sense to end the reign of the monsters chasing us all down a dark hall. You are empowered. Nothing is going to happen to you for peaking beyond the curtain into truth.

Fear is the greatest tool in enslaving this world. Challenge the fear. Speak your truth. Feed diversity. Challenge a vengeful and petty God. In doing that, you will break through to the freedom of absolute empowerment of divine love and acceptance. It is the means to free the struggling masses. They have no more to learn by being left alone in their plight. That is another layer of lies to protect the illusion. It is enforced in the subtle realms and holds those, who would otherwise be spiritually free, in a subtle haze of superiority.

We have all done this dance so much that the only thing new to learn is that we are indeed all one. When we free others, we are not interfering with their karma. We are freeing ourselves of our own dross because we are all prisms in the same light. They are reflecting a fragment of ourselves back to us. By overcoming everything that we have been told (even in our secret doctrines), and choosing love and kindness, we choose self-empowerment.

What I write is sanctioned by the Ancient Ones. They are not owned or copyrighted to any agenda. Their sacred trust has been bastardized for a few petty baubles in the play of power. I have no agenda in writing it. I am not even certain of what I am going to write when I start. I just know that I have endured and been kept alive to share with you now. I have nothing to lose in doing so. I also have nothing to gain. It is humanity that gains in knowing these things. May my writings be a pathway to you finding the awakening of truth in yourself and in all of us.

9: ABOLISHING RACISM

We are sadly disappointed here in America if we expect our "leaders" to bring an end to racism. It is not a black and white issue. It is a humanity issue. Racism is formed when an individual or a group is disappointed in itself and projects that disappointment onto another group. Racism is a form of self-loathing. This is unbearable for people to tolerate so they spew that internal pressure onto a targeted demographic.

Racism as we see it today is an echo of a deeply disturbing time many times in history. What is happening now in the world is that humanity is being cleansed of all its old engrams which are habitual behaviors from the past. We are all seeing them paraded before us in the ugly behavior, politics and lack of civility seen in interactions. But it is only a temporary issue.

Racism will not be allowed to entrench into the fibers of humanity. We are all just witnessing the horrific reminders of it before it is to die away altogether. Ignorance and intolerance will go the way of the eight-track. They will both die an unceremonious death. It is actually what we are all witnessing. Racism and ignorance are taking their last dramatic gasping breath. Witnessing it will allow all of humanity to be grateful for being free of it.

Racism is psychic energy that is organically brewed. It is easy to create psychic energy if you can muster enough fear and hate. Both are the key ingredients to creating and sustaining such noxious psychic atmosphere. There is so much love on the planet and more pouring in every day that it is impossible for hate to sustain itself here. We are watching the last stubborn hoarders of hate blow their last wad.

I know it doesn't seem like it to those who are in the trenches dealing with prejudice. But please know, as much as the "ignorant" work to muster up more hate, there are those "Love Workers" like myself dampening the flames at every turn. In fact, the most devastating hate is not a match for the sincere presence of dynamic, intentional kindness and compassion. It has a healing quality. This is the balm that I send out to the world with all my abilities and intentions. It is what I teach others to do through my writings and retreats and exercises.

The techniques that I share can be very effective in addressing a cause. They are able to use mind energy that is not consciously utilized to bring about an incredible shift in dynamics. It is relatively easy to dissipate psychic energy. It is a matter of doing it from a far away vantage point so as not to get immersed in it. It is similar to fighting a blazing fire from outside of it. Getting caught up in the emotions of any issue is like choking on the smoke of a fire. That is why this exercise can be so effective. It is addressing the issue without getting immersed in the psychic energy.

Here is a technique for every individual to dissipate racism. As we have experienced, the cure doesn't happen in the streets. Or, it hasn't dissipated in the streets since the likes of the great soul Martin Luther King, Jr. What he did was access a pure conviction fueled by passion to ignite others into his conviction. His success was fueled by the emotional turmoil of the time. What I am doing here is similar, but it is on a more subtle level. I am using my abilities as a shaman (energy mover) to dissipate the energies of hate by drying them up with a pure intention of love. It is no different than the sunshine drying up the storm clouds.

In fact, that is a great visualization for people who are good at visualizations. In contemplation, see the earth from the vantage point of far away, as if you were in a spaceship. See the dark clouds of hate that have been brewing. Notice they have even been getting darker recently with the rhetoric and frustration of groups of haters. Now, simply surround the planet in your love. If you don't know how to do this, simply imagine yourself as the sun and emanate beautiful rays onto the planet.

Watch all the clouds dry up. See how you are not getting caught up in the emotional component of the issue or thinking too much. Thought energy and emotional energy help the storm clouds brew. Sending detached love rays to all dissipates them. Even if only one reader joins me in doing this visualization, the world can be uplifted by the effects.

I implore as many people as possible to add their loving intention to this important cause by doing this exercise. They can also do the set of taps I post below. This is a great set of taps to do as an introduction to this powerful technique. Imagine how silly the first people trying yoga may have felt, and now yoga is now a mainstay of society. Tapping will be a mainstay in the future. It is training the neglected humans what their empowerment is capable of achieving.

Tapping is a very powerful means of utilizing your mind energy that the ego prevents us from accessing otherwise. The tapping process bypasses the ego. I can't think of a better set of taps to introduce someone to tapping. If it is your first set of taps, pay attention to sensations in your body like yawning or heaviness. These are evidence that something is releasing when you do these taps.

Please say each statement slowly and deliberately as if

you are commanding the Universe to oblige because you are. Say each statement a total of four times before moving on to the next. Say it three times while continuously tapping on the top of your head at the point of your soft spot or crown chakra. Say it a fourth time while tapping the middle of your chest. The first three times will be shifting your mind to manifest the command of the tap. The fourth time is setting it in the body so the mind continues on the trajectory of the new intention. Also, say them matter of fact without passion or drama. That only deters from their effectiveness. Do them in a robotic way.

The first tap will be said as "I." But the ones after that will be said as "We" because you are not doing this exercise alone. You are adding your synergy to all the other readers who are doing this exercise as well. It is a subtle but very effective way of addressing the currents of racism that are seemingly going unchecked. Feel the validation in doing this. Feel the connection to others. Feel the effectiveness on a deep level. Then after sharing with as many people as possible, simply watch the results play out. It can be that simple. It is a time for racism to die out on the planet, and this is your opportunity to be a part of it. It is also the answer to many prayers.

Remember: Say each statement three times while tapping on your head and then say it a fourth time while tapping on your chest. Pause before "in all

moments."

"I declare myself a surrogate for humanity in doing these taps; in all moments."

"We dry up all the psychic energy of racism; in all moments."

"We release feeding racism with fear or hate; in all moments."

"We dry up all fear and hate; in all moments"

"We release projecting our unworthiness onto others; in all moments."

"We release using others as a scapegoat for our own lack; in all moments."

"We release demonizing one race; in all moments."

"We release all entitlement that causes a reaction to others; in all moments."

"We nullify all contracts with racism; in all moments."

"We release being in competition with others; in all moments."

"We shift the Universal paradigm from the human race to the Human Being; in all moments."

"We release the genetic propensity to be racist; in all moments."

"We release the cultural propensity to be a racist; in all moments."

"We remove all vortexes between ourselves and racism; in all moments."

"We release being ruled by a racist agenda; in all moments."

"We remove all tentacles between ourselves and racism; in all moments."

"We eliminate the first cause in regard to racism; in all moments."

"We strip all illusion off of racism; in all moments."

"We strip all masks, walls and armor off of all racists; in all moments."

"We collapse and dissolve all portals to racism; in all moments."

"We shatter all glass ceilings that racism has put on us; in all moments."

"We remove all tentacles between ourselves and all racism; in all moments."

"We dry up all Akashic records of racism; in all moments."

"We remove all programming and conditioning that racism has put on us; in all moments."

"We remove all engrams of racism; in all moments."

"We send all energy matrices into the Light and Sound that perpetuate or support racism; in all moments."

"We command all complex energy matrices that perpetuate or support racism to be escorted into the Light and Sound; in all moments."

"We recant all vows and agreements between ourselves and racism; in all moments."

"We remove all curses between ourselves and racism; in all moments."

"We remove all blessings between ourselves and racism; in all moments."

"We sever all strings, cords, and chains between ourselves and racism; in all moments."

"We release being enslaved to racism; in all moments."

"We dissolve all karmic ties between ourselves and racism; in all moments."

"We remove all the pain, burden, limitations, anger, fear, unworthiness, rejection, futility and illusion of separateness that racism has put on us; in all moments."

"We take back all the joy, love, abundance, freedom, health, success, security, companionship, creativity, peace, life, wholeness, beauty, enthusiasm, contentment, spirituality, enlightenment, contentment, intellect, ability to discern, confidence and empowerment that racism has taken from us; in all moments."

"We shift our paradigm from racism to Universal Joy, Love, Abundance and Freedom; in all moments."

"We release resonating or emanating with racism; in all moments."

"We extract all racism from our Sound Frequency and our Light Emanation; in all moments."

"We transcend racism; in all moments."

"We are centered and empowered in Universal Joy, Love, Abundance and Freedom; in all moments."

"We infuse Joy, Love, Abundance and Freedom into our Universal Sound Frequency and Light Emanation; in all moments."

"We resonate, emanate, and are interconnected with all life in Universal Joy, Love, Abundance and Freedom; in all moments."

I know it may seem silly to do these taps if it is your first time. But this is my skill set. I would not be able to motivate you to rally. That is not what I do. I am using my innate talents to bring about an effective change in humanity. Isn't that what we are all here to do? Imagine if everyone were simply encouraged to share their gifts. How the world would be different. May all people get back to the simple grace of sharing their gifts.

10: FROM CONGRESS TO INTEGRITY

A client and friend who does the taps I post religiously had a telling dream. She was in a huge dilapidated house that was falling apart. The siding was off on one side and it was in ruins. But she was trapped inside. She couldn't get out because she was trapped in a contract with this house and was obligated to own it. She felt hopeless. In the dream, she was told to do a set of taps to free her from all obligations to this house.

When she awoke, she knew that the dream was referring to the House of Congress. She is so close to me and I am so energetically busy, the Guides sometimes give her messages for me. This was one of those dreams. These taps are effective. We are seeing it in people voicing their individuality instead of sitting helplessly by. These taps are a means to gain empowerment for all of humanity without putting one's self out there in the usual way that has set them up for demise through history.

In another part of the dream, my friend saw all these different sections of the house with red strips of tape on it. She started pulling off all the red tape. She took this to mean literal red tape; I saw it as red state bias. Regardless, it is a good visualization to pull all the red tape off. It was her dream. So her interpretation prevails.

(Say each statement three times while tapping on your head and say it a fourth time while tapping on your chest. Then go on to the next.)

"I declare myself a surrogate for humanity in doing these taps; in all moments."

"We strip all denial off of the world in dealing with Congress; in all moments."

"We release allowing Congress to interfere with personal freedom; in all moments."

"We dissipate the systemic indifference that allows Congress to limit the quality of life for all; in all moments."

"We remove all masks, walls, and armor off of the use of Congress; in all moments."

"We remove all masks, walls, and armor off of using Congress to elect unqualified officials; in all moments."

"We release allowing Congress to strip individuals' civil liberties; in all moments."

"We prevent members of Congress from wielding

personal power; in all moments."

"We prevent Congress from wielding power for big business; in all moments."

"We release allowing Congress to diminish our freedom of choice; in all moments."

"We release passively watching while big business buys and sells Congress; in all moments."

"We strip all illusion off of Congress; in all moments."

"We release being indifferent or apathetic to Congress; in all moments."

"We release being separated from our humanity by Congress; in all moments."

"We release being manipulated by Congress; in all moments."

"We release deferring to Congress in all things sacred; in all moments."

"We release allowing Congress to frame society's conception of Source; in all moments."

"We release allowing Congress to shove an agenda down our throat; in all moments."

"We break up the cluster of power mongers that use Congress to diminish others; in all moments."

"We release being kept in ignorance by Congress; in all moments."

"We release being duped by Congress; in all moments."

"We release adulating members of Congress; in all moments."

"We release being stripped of our progressiveness by Congress; in all moments."

"We release being complacent with the manipulative ploys of Congress; in all moments."

"We release having our humanity gutted by Congress; in all moments."

"We release the worship of Congress; in all moments."

"We eliminate the first cause in the diversion of Congress from its original intention; in all moments."

"We release being deceived by Congress; in all moments."

"We strip all illusion and defenses off those who use Congress to control others; in all moments."

"We release converting our sacred devotion to God into deference to Congress; in all moments."

"We release being enslaved to Congress; in all moments."

"We release diminishing ourselves by allowing Congress to mandate civil liberties; in all moments."

"We remove all vivaxes between ourselves and Congress; in all moments."

"We remove all tentacles between ourselves and Congress; in all moments."

"We withdraw all our energy from Congress; in all moments."

"We release having blind faith in Congress; in all moments."

"We collapse and dissolve all opportunities to use Congress for personal gain; in all moments."

"We remove all programming and conditioning that Congress has put on us; in all moments."

"We remove all individual and universal engrams of Congress; in all moments."

"We release allowing Congress to entangle us by using our sacred doctrines; in all moments."

"We release allowing Congress to rob us of our voice; in all moments."

"We release the belief that Congress is beyond reproach; in all moments."

"We send all energy matrices into the light and sound

that enable Congress to diminish civil liberties; in all moments."

"We command all complex energy matrices that enable Congress to diminish civil liberties to be escorted into the light and sound; in all moments."

"We send all energy matrices into the light and sound that blind us to abuses of power of Congress; in all moments."

"We command all complex energy matrices that blind us to abuses of power of Congress to be escorted into the light and sound; in all moments."

"We send all energy matrices into the light and sound that prevent us from cleaning up Congress; in all moments."

"We command all complex energy matrices that prevent us from cleaning up Congress to be escorted into the light and sound; in all moments."

"We release being deceived by Congress; in all moments."

"We recant all vows and agreements between ourselves and Congress; in all moments."

"We remove all curses between ourselves and Congress; in all moments."

"We remove all blessings between ourselves and

Congress; in all moments."

"We remove all payoffs to all those who use Congress to profit, wield power or peddle an ignoble agenda; in all moments."

"We sever all strings, cords and psychic connection between ourselves and all members of Congress; in all moments."

"We sever all strings, cords and psychic connection between ourselves and Congress; in all moments."

"We dissipate all psychic streams of energy that allow Congress to go unchecked; in all moments."

"We dissolve all karmic ties between ourselves and Congress; in all moments."

"We remove all the pain, burden, limitations, fear, futility, unworthiness and illusion of separateness that Congress has put on us; in all moments."

"We bury Congress in the weight of its own ignoble intentions; in all moments."

"We remove all muscle memory that causes us to defer to Congress; in all moments."

"We dismantle all energy grids between ourselves and Congress; in all moments."

"We take back all the joy, love, abundance, freedom,

health, success, security, companionship, creativity, peace, life, wholeness, beauty, enthusiasm, contentment, spirituality, enlightenment, confidence, ability to discern and empowerment that Congress has taken from us; in all moments."

"We disarm the ability of Congress to desecrate earth; in all moments."

"We disarm the ability of Congress to strip individuals of their civil liberties; in all moments."

"We strip Congress of its illusion of propriety; in all moments."

"We strip Congress of its illusion of hiding behind the noble intention of our founding fathers; in all moments."

"We disarm Congress from the ability to dwindle our life, liberties and pursuit of happiness; in all moments."

"We crumble and dissolve all constructs created by Congress; in all moments."

"We nullify all contracts with Congress; in all moments."

"We strip all illusion off those who benefit from using Congress to wield power or gain wealth; in all moments."

"We eliminate the first cause in all mandates of an

ignoble Congress; in all moments."

"We hold open a portal for Universal integrity in all; in all moments."

"We release confusing Congress with the original integrity of the founding fathers; in all moments."

"We release confusing Congress with the original greatness of the founding fathers; in all moments."

"We release resonating or emanating with Congress; in all moments."

"We extract all of the limitations of Congress from our individual and Universal Sound Frequency; in all moments."

"We extract all of the limitations of Congress from our individual and Universal Light Emanation; in all moments."

"We extract all of the limitations of Congress from all 32 layers of our individual and Universal aura; in all moments."

"We extract all of the limitations of Congress from our whole beingness; in all moments."

"We shift our paradigm from Congress to individual and Universal joy, love, abundance, freedom, health, peace, strength, empowerment, and integrity; in all moments."

"We transcend Congress; in all moments."

"We are centered and empowered in integrity; in all moments."

"We infuse integrity into our sound frequency; in all moments."

"We imbue integrity into our light emanation; in all moments."

"We resonate, emanate and are interconnected to all life integrity; in all moments."

If you are from another country, you can use the word that fits your governing branch, the world parliament perhaps. Thank you.

11: WHAT IS BEING INFUSED BACK INTO HUMANITY?

About a week ago, I awoke exhausted. Fortunately, I am conscious when I need to be on the other side of sleep and knew why. It was an all night celebration. There was a parade. There were soldiers from every war who had come home. War had ended in the world and all the souls who were trapped in dying in war were free and whole again.

Perhaps now veterans can heal. Perhaps you were there celebrating and woke up tired too. It is okay. So many souls have been waiting for this particular lifetime when this would occur. Feeling tired and lethargic is a small price to pay now that you realize why. And now you can be reassured there will be no more war. No matter what a sprinkling of buffoons wish.

I just woke up from a dream where there was a bunch of older kids (enthusiasm) in a craft store (creativity). They were having fun. Nothing mean spirited. But it was a lighthearted game (life). I had to go find a material to make an outfit for my bear (reconstruct my physical self). We were all playing the game (humanity), but they were all peaking around the corner seeing what I would choose first (being inspired and encouraged by me).

All the while, a tune was playing over the speakers as back ground music (being piped into humanity). It was Kermit the frog (innocence) singing a Mister Rogers (trustworthy) song. The song basically repeated two stanzas. The song said, "I messed up but I forgive myself because I matter." It was being pumped into humanity by those who are assisting in raising the consciousness of humanity.

I was being shown how the deep engrams of shame and unworthiness are being worked out of people while they sleep. We are creating a construct for our new selves in a vibration that already exists and that permeates us. But we can only perceive it from a level of accepting ourselves and feeling worthy. Shame, false humility and guilt do not resonate with the higher frequencies. They are like oil and water.

We all need to love ourselves and others more to assist everyone in raising their vibration so that they can perceive in higher consciousness. It is already here. We merely have to elevate ourselves to accept the level of love that it offers. Notice the reality on TV is nothing like the reality when you walk outside on a beautiful day? Accept the latter as your truth and it will help to quicken the igniting of mass awakening.

When I woke up, I could not get back to sleep. The TV is flashing an error on the box. It is reminding me that the news and what is on TV is not reality and is merely being used to help all those who are still on the fence about awakening to be brought up to speed. They are getting a crash course viewing the abuse of power. The TV box is rebooting. This is what humanity is doing. We are rebooting to be more attuned with peace, kindness, awareness, integrity and love.

Me writing this is me back in the craft store assisting in the construct of higher consciousness. You reading this are the happy playful children peeking around the corner. Such is the synchronicity and serendipity of life and love. We are immersed in the more subtle realms as much as we allow ourselves to accept it. Remember the song. We have all messed up. But we forgive ourselves.

12: FOSSIL FUEL

The fossil fuel monopoly is how the oligarchies plan to dissect the world into their personal markets. The whole reason that the conservatives don't believe in climate change is because they have been manipulated by billionaires who use God and the Bible to keep people ignorant to the fact that THEY WANT the icecaps to melt so they can harvest untapped resources under the ground there. You can tell if any group has been tainted by greed or manipulated by greed if they believe that there is no climate change. Either they directly benefit, are in the pocket of someone who directly benefits, or are easily manipulated by propaganda or rhetoric by those who benefit.

All the technologies of the great thinkers have been bought up by billionaires so we don't benefit from what is possible. I never realized where global warming fit into this until watching the news recently and seeing the interest that both Donald Trump and Russia have in drilling under the Arctic now that the icecaps are melting. I just thought the billionaires were indifferent to whether crops could grow because when the world became too scorched for natural growing seasons, they could swoop in like heroes with their GMO's and save the day. They are much more sinister and selfish than that. They want to rape the land of all natural resources as well.

A couple of short years ago, this kind of talk would seem like conspiracy theory gibberish. But thanks to Donald Trump, we are all too savvy to overlook the possibilities. We seem to be sitting by and watching it happen. But those who are doing the taps I post on my page realize that we are energetically addressing the takers on subtle levels that they have tried so desperately to keep us ignorant of. The taps I post and the energy work I do are working in accordance with such truth as is depicted in the trailer on the movie, *Thrive*.

When I watch the news, truth opens up to me of what is happening on subtle levels, even on sinister levels. As so many people are wondering, "Why Trump? What is going on?" truth opened up to me, and it was chilling. Putin is working with China to dismantle America. Putin has Trump in his pocket like a stooge. Trump is playing his part. Putin manipulated the Syrian attack and told Trump what to do to put distance between them. But Trump is just a dupe. It is actually the

American billionaires who are working with the Russian oligarchy billionaires to dismantle America so the world can be run by the oligarchies of the world unhampered by country divides.

Putin was the black magician, Rasputin, in a past life. Rasputin is the one who took the healing arts and convinced the world that they were all evil. He is the one who imbued his future incarnation with such psychic and manipulative powers. Only a person with the understanding of the skills of Rasputin could remove the spell he put on people in his future incarnation as Putin. This has been the source of Putin's power. Not this lifetime, but in his lifetime as Rasputin.

I am the reincarnation of Madame Blavatsky. When I was much younger, I was told that I was she but did not want to believe it because she was so homely. A couple of years back I was holding her image next to mine, and my cousin's jaw dropped. The likeness is uncanny. My ability to be prolific in writing is further evidence. Many people have had their own personal revelations of me being she. They will be drawn to her and find me, not realizing why, until they understand the connection.

I have evolved into owning an incredible ability that lay hidden under a very miserable life. Every time I was brought to a dynamic healer, they would tell me the same thing. Although I had no money to pay, they were instructed by their Guides to do everything in their power to assist me in getting empowered. I am empowered. I went through enlightenment over nine years ago when I was held in captivity. It was orchestrated on some level. Since then, I have been living as a recluse like a monk, writing prolifically in different ways to help people find their own empowerment, waiting until I was strong enough to be seen as the empowered being I have become. The time is now. The world needs us all to gain our empowerment and stop playing the victim. The stakes are too high.

The Guides have been giving me a means to teach people how to quickly and efficiently regain their empowerment through a tapping protocol they have instructed me to put together. It is called SFT and stands for Spiritual Freedom Technique. Because that is what it truly is. So many have already gained empowerment through using the taps. The protocol is a series of affirmations done while tapping the brain and then the chest while repeating. It works because the tapping instructs the brain to give the statement first priority in manifesting what the conscious mind commands. That is the beauty of the brain that humans just can't seem to realize. The brain will manifest everything we tell it to the letter. We just have been programmed to tell it such negative things to manifest, which it obliges.

A group of dynamic people have gotten together with

me to do a series of tapping protocols to benefit humanity. We have addressed many psychic forms of manipulation that most people would have thought ridiculous a short time ago. But through the stripping off of the psychic layers of manipulation that humanity has been immersed in, through the tapping, more and more people are awake enough to discern the truth.

A couple of things worth noting about the tapping protocol: I assist all individuals and groups with creating the great shift they feel in doing the taps, and I assist in dissipating the stagnant energy that is a by-product. Also, the taps are designed for individuals to withdraw all their energy from groups that have stripped them of their empowerment. These are the groups that have used it as a building block to limit, beguile or even rape humanity in some way. It is no different than the conservatives being used as numbers to keep Trump able to dismantle civil liberties. But in a couple of generations, after people become accustomed to tapping to maintain their center, tapping will no longer be necessary. Future generations will simply understand the power of their intentions and the importance of the vibration of their words and even thoughts.

Another really important thing to know to reassure people is that I formulated a set of taps that has been used to strip Rasputin of his ability to control people. We have dismantled the energetic power source to

Putin's reign. The world is being put back on track for individual empowerment and freedom. It took a dynamic Energy worker to dissipate all the energy of the black magician.

Now, hopefully, the world can awaken from the stupor and accept the truth in the trailer on the movie *Thrive*. Now they can accept their part and realize how important it is that they hold space for a higher vibration on the planet. It can be done simply by taking in the information that is presented here and accepting the truth that has been here all along.

Power, greed and the spell that had us worshipping monetary wealth have been broken. It is time for you to hold a higher vibration in your atoms. It is ridiculous at this point to deny doing so.

Please watch the trailer below.
https://www.youtube.com/watch?v=OibqdwHyZxk

13: MANY HANDS

Some of my posts are controversial, and I know that they may create disturbance, but they are what the Guides who assist me tell me to share. It doesn't matter if they are received well at the time; they are poking a hole in the consciousness for a greater truth.

Poking through the consciousness of earth is like trying to dig a well that fills in on itself. Continuing to press through is an unrelenting task, but it must be done for truth to take hold. That is why it is so appreciated when others share my posts. They are assisting in digging through the apathy and denial and allowing a means for pure truth to well up. It is not enough for one shovel to dig through. Everyone must join in and scoop out the dross that prevents all from partaking of truth.

Today I wrote a piece about how propagation of the species is being manipulated by those who have an agenda. We are manipulated into feeling obligated to procreate without any concern to how we are plowing through natural resources. I explained that having children to multiply the earth is man's law, not God's. I wrote how life is eternal and doesn't begin by rubbing two clay pots together. Those two clay pots can only create another clay pot, a temporary house for the eternal. Soul is eternal. God breathed soul into the body of Adam after he formed his body out of dust.

I was explaining how the Guides want me to share stark naked truth so that it can poke that initial hole through to more truth. I was thinking of this and beginning to type a message to someone. Instead of writing a salutation or a light greeting, my fingers typed out two words on their own: THANK YOU. I looked unbelieving at what I myself just wrote. I believe my Guides were using my own hand to type their appreciation to me. It was a profound moment. They had me type the words "thank you."

I will continue to share what they ask. I will continue to appreciate those who share.

Transcending the Dark Ages

I am stretching my energy out wider to reach a global audience rather than national. This is really exciting. It means that the world is more ready to accept truth and I am strong enough to stay centered as I share the insights that are pumped through me by Ancient Teachers.

They are so pleased that the earth is accepting truth as it is. Even though outer conditions may make it seem otherwise, truth is being heard, accepted and realized. The fact that it looks like such a mess is an exciting thing. When was earth untainted in modern times? The fact that the majority is privy to the profound depth of deceit that has been earth's mainstay is profound.

We are finally and realistically just now emerging from the dark ages. So many of you can see that now. As much as it is a pain to figure out how to support my posts on my blog, I would appreciate your presence there. You have been my dearest companions on this journey. I would love to be surrounded by your encouragement as we all transcend together into enlightenment.

14: FREEING THE WORLD OF A DARK FORCE

The Dali Lama said that the world will be saved by a western woman. He was referring to the work we do here. It is obvious to so many that Putin is working to take over the world. The way our own government sits by and watches him wear our government like a well-fitted puppet is unfathomable. Yes, we are all watching aghast as that happens.

The reason the world seems to be powerless against stopping Putin is because he is the reincarnation of Rasputin. Rasputin was a nineteenth century monk who was known as a mystic. He used healing techniques to endear himself to the Czar of Russia and won great favor. But he used dark arts. He turned healing into a negative practice and entrenched himself into a powerful position using black magic.

I get the sense he learned his abilities by learning from Madame Blavatsky's teachings. She only wanted to empower the world with truth and it was used for ignoble purposes. Putin is not really the problem in enslaving the masses. It is his incarnation as Rasputin that is wielding power through its future incarnation of Putin. So if you want to undo the hold that Putin has on the world, you address his lifetime as a mystic when he poured his dark intentions into the world. Those are the ones that hold the key to usurping Putin.

It makes perfect sense that a Russian mystic and dynamic healer from the past (Madame Blavatsky) would be the one to dissipate the scourge on the earth that a Russian self-proclaimed mystic from the past (Rasputin) cursed the world with. Those who get a sense of this truth will be thrilled to participate in the freeing of humanity in doing these taps.

(Say each statement three times while tapping on your head and say it a fourth time while tapping on your chest. Then go on to the next.)

"I declare myself a surrogate for humanity in doing these taps; in all moments."

"We strip all denial off of the world in dealing with Rasputin; in all moments."

"We release allowing Rasputin to enslave humanity; in all moments."

"We dissipate the dark psychic energy that allows Rasputin to control the world; in all moments."

"We remove all masks, walls, and armor off the workings of Rasputin; in all moments."

"We expose Putin as the long arm of Rasputin; in all moments."

"We release allowing Rasputin to rule the world; in all moments"

"We release allowing Rasputin to strip humanity of its ability to discern; in all moments."

"We protect all individuals from being affected by Rasputin; in all moments."

"We stop Rasputin from pimping out humanity for his own pleasure; in all moments."

"We stop Rasputin from wielding power through oligarchies; in all moments."

"We stop Rasputin from hiding his deceit; in all moments."

"We release allowing Rasputin to own our freedom; in all moments."

"We release passively watching while Rasputin takes over the world; in all moments."

"We strip all illusion off of Rasputin; in all moments."

"We release being duped into giving our passion to Rasputin; in all moments."

"We release being separated from our humanity by Rasputin; in all moments."

"We release being manipulated by Rasputin; in all moments."

"We release deferring to Rasputin in all things sacred; in all moments."

"We release allowing Rasputin to frame our perception of reality; in all moments."

"We release allowing Rasputin to shove an agenda down our throat; in all moments."

"We dissolve Rasputin's dark intentions to rule the world; in all moments."

"We release being kept in ignorance by Rasputin; in all moments."

"We release being duped by Rasputin; in all moments."

"We release adulating Rasputin; in all moments."

"We release engaging Rasputin; in all moments."

"We release being stripped of our inclusiveness by Rasputin; in all moments."

"We release being complacent in dealing with Rasputin; in all moments."

"We release the fear of Rasputin; in all moments."

"We release having our humanity gutted by Rasputin; in all moments."

"We release being pimped into a hellish existence by Rasputin; in all moments."

"We eliminate the first cause in Rasputin gaining power; in all moments."

"We release being immersed in the psychic energies of Rasputin; in all moments."

"We strip all illusion and defenses off those who serve Rasputin; in all moments."

"We release converting our sacred devotion to God into deference to Rasputin; in all moments."

"'We release being enslaved to Rasputin; in all moments."

"We release diminishing ourselves by allowing Rasputin to hold our attention; in all moments."

"We remove all vivaxes between ourselves and Rasputin; in all moments."

"We remove all tentacles between ourselves and Rasputin; in all moments."

"We withdraw all our energy from Rasputin; in all moments."

"We release being naïve to Rasputin; in all moments."

"We collapse and dissolve all constructs of Rasputin; in all moments."

"We remove all programming and conditioning that Rasputin has put on us; in all moments."

"We remove all individual and universal engrams of Rasputin from our whole beingness; in all moments."

"We remove all controlling devices that Rasputin has put on us; in all moments."

"We release allowing Rasputin to induce us to fear or hatred; in all moments."

"We release allowing Rasputin to rob us of our voice or dignity; in all moments."

"We release the belief that abiding by Rasputin is inevitable; in all moments."

"We send all energy matrices into the light and sound that enable Rasputin; in all moments."

"We command all complex energy matrices that enable Rasputin be escorted into the light and sound; in all moments."

"We send all energy matrices into the light and sound that make up the psychic forces of Rasputin; in all moments."

"We command all complex energy matrices that make up the psychic forces of Rasputin to be escorted into the light and sound; in all moments."

"We send all energy matrices into the light and sound that perpetuate the ignoble intentions of Rasputin; in all moments."

"We command all complex energy matrices that perpetuate the ignoble intentions of Rasputin to be escorted into the light and sound; in all moments."

"We release being deceived by the ignoble intentions of Rasputin; in all moments."

"We nullify all contacts with Rasputin; in all moments."

"We recant all vows and agreements between ourselves and Rasputin; in all moments."

"We remove all curses between ourselves and Rasputin; in all moments."

"We remove all curses that Rasputin has put on the world; in all moments."

"We remove all blessings between ourselves and Rasputin; in all moments."

"We remove all payoffs to all those who support Rasputin; in all moments."

"We sever all strings, cords and psychic connection between ourselves and Rasputin; in all moments."

"We sever all strings, cords and psychic connection between ourselves and all those who support Rasputin;

in all moments."

"We dissipate all psychic streams of energy that Rasputin has allowed to go unchecked; in all moments."

"We dissolve all karmic ties between ourselves and Rasputin; in all moments."

"We remove all the pain, burden, limitations, fear, futility, unworthiness, anger, abandonment, rejection and illusion of separateness that Rasputin has put on us; in all moments."

"We bury Rasputin in the weight of his own ignoble intentions; in all moments."

"We remove all muscle memory of deferring to Rasputin; in all moments."

"We break all energy grids between ourselves and Rasputin; in all moments."

"We take back all the joy, love, abundance, freedom, health, success, security, companionship, creativity, peace, life, wholeness, beauty, enthusiasm, contentment, spirituality, enlightenment, confidence, ability to discern, individuality and empowerment that Rasputin has taken from us; in all moments."

"We disarm the ability of Rasputin to desecrate earth; in all moments."

"We disarm the ability of Rasputin to enslave humanity;

in all moments."

"We strip Rasputin of its illusion; in all moments."

"We strip Rasputin of its authority; in all moments."

"We disarm Rasputin from the ability to dwindle our quality of life; in all moments."

"We eliminate the first cause in Rasputin tainting the healing arts; in all moments."

"We crumble and dissolve all constructs created by Rasputin; in all moments."

'We nullify all contracts with the constructs of Rasputin; in all moments."

"We strip all illusion off those who benefit from supporting Rasputin; in all moments."

"We eliminate the first cause in all the mandates of Rasputin; in all moments."

"We hold open all portals for higher consciousness and Universal peace in all; in all moments."

"We release confusing Rasputin with integrity; in all moments."

"We release confusing Rasputin with inevitability; in all moments."

"We release resonating or emanating with Rasputin; in

all moments."

"We extract all of Rasputin from our individual and Universal Sound Frequency; in all moments."

"We extract all of Rasputin from our individual and Universal Light Emanation; in all moments."

"We extract all of Rasputin from all 32 layers of our individual and Universal aura; in all moments."

"We extract all of Rasputin from our whole beingness; in all moments."

"We blast pure all aspects of the world that Rasputin tainted; in all moments."

"We shift our paradigm from Rasputin to the higher consciousness of individual and universal joy, love, abundance, freedom, health, peace, strength, empowerment and integrity; in all moments."

"We transcend Rasputin; in all moments."

"We are centered and empowered in the higher consciousness of Universal Peace; in all moments."

"We infuse the higher consciousness of Universal Peace into our Sound frequency; in all moments."

"We imbue the higher consciousness of Universal Peace into our Light emanation; in all moments."

"We resonate, emanate and are interconnected to all life

in the higher consciousness of Universal Peace; in all moments."

15: LOWEST COMMON DENOMINATOR

Politics is one of the most negative experiences we have on this planet. It is where manipulation, greed and guile put on a sweet face to manipulate those who are trusting.

Think of the place where hot and cold meet to create condensation and form a cloud. The cloud that the negativity of politics forms in coming against the truth of higher consciousness leaves us all in a fog. The negativity of politics must be tempered so when it meets the truth of our gaining innate goodness, the cloud is less dense. The experience is softened for all involved. At this point, all of humanity is involved.

It is a shame that political movements target people with simple values who love God and are trying to be good people. They are fed lies and distorted into hating machines that are defensive and unable to receive truth. They don't realize that the people who are feeding them the agenda are paid henchmen of the movement. They are being duped.

Those of us who are too savvy to agree are demonized as the opposition party, which most of us are not.

It is a shame when political factions desecrate truth and abuse an untarnished person to attain such a desecration of freedom. This is what is being witnessed by so many currently. You know how to tell? Someone spends their lifetime doing what they love. You know how you can tell someone has integrity? Both sides of an issue disagree with them and yet both sides of the aisle respect them as well. It turns my stomach that the playbook in politics is intending to smear someone's reputation. It is shameful.

So I am compelled to share this energetic technique to dismantle the psychic manipulation that is used to desecrate goodness.

Those in a majority many times seize any disadvantaged situation to push their slanted policies onto mainstream.

(Say each statement three times while tapping on your head and say it a fourth time while tapping on your chest.)

"I declare myself a surrogate for humanity in doing these taps; in all moments."

"We release being held hostage by the lowest common denominator; in all moments."

"We convert the hate that drives the lowest common denominator into discernment; in all moments."

"We dry up the psychic manipulation that feeds the lowest common denominator; in all moments."

"We strip all illusion off of those who prop up the lowest common denominator; in all moments."

"We prevent the lowest common denominator in gaining any negative traction; in all moments."

"We dissipate the ability for the lowest common denominator to wilt the bloom of Truth in the world; in all moments."

"We release being overtaken by the likes of the lowest common denominator; in all moments."

"We untangle all individuals from the lowest common denominator; in all moments."

"We strip all illusion off of the lowest common denominator; in all moments."

"We prevent the lowest common denominator from perpetuating a false narrative; in all moments."

"We free all individuals from the lowest common denominator; in all moments."

"We nullify all agreements with the lowest common denominator; in all moments."

"We remove all tentacles between ourselves and the lowest common denominator; in all moments."

"We remove all programing and conditioning that the lowest common denominator has put on us; in all moments."

"We remove all engrams of the lowest common denominator from our beingness; in all moments."

"We eliminate the first cause in the creation of the lowest common denominator; in all moments."

"We send all energy matrices into the Light and Sound that advocate for the lowest common denominator; in all moments."

"We command all complex energy matrices that advocate for the lowest common denominator to be escorted into the Light and Sound; in all moments."

"We shatter all glass ceilings that the lowest common denominator has put on us; in all moments."

"We collapse and dissolve all portals to the lowest common denominator; in all moments."

"We recant all vows and agreements between ourselves and the lowest common denominator; in all moments."

"We remove all curses between ourselves and the lowest common denominator; in all moments."

"We remove all blessings between ourselves and the lowest common denominator; in all moments."

"We withdraw all our energy from the lowest common denominator; in all moments."

"We sever all strings, cords and psychic connections between ourselves and the lowest common denominator; in all moments."

"We dissolve all karmic ties between ourselves and the lowest common denominator; in all moments."

"We remove all the pain, burden and limitations that the lowest common denominator has put on us; in all moments."

"We take back all that the lowest common denominator has taken from us; in all moments."

"We release resonating or emanating with the lowest common denominator; in all moments."

"We extract all of the lowest common denominator from our Sound Frequency; in all moments."

"We extract all of the lowest common denominator from our Light emanation; in all moments."

"We shift our paradigm from the lowest common denominator to individualized Freedom, Love and Truth; in all moments."

"We transcend the lowest common denominator; in all moments."

"We are centered and empowered in individualized Freedom, Love and Truth; in all moments."

"We resonate, emanate and are interconnected with all life in individualized Freedom, Love and Truth; in all moments."

Even one person doing these taps with intention and sincerity can change the course of our outcome. May it be you.

16: CLEANING THE SLATE OF ALL OLD ENGRAMS

Most people don't realize it, but we are not existing in the third dimension anymore. We have transcended to the fifth dimension. We did so without much fanfare or the need for a mass exodus by souls who aren't able to handle the shift. They are being coddled in a way because they were allowed to bring their baggage from the lower states of consciousness with them until they are able to let go of it on their own. It is much kinder this way than to have it ripped away in a stringent upgrade.

There is evidence of the shift in consciousness in subtle ways: Fear, war and power plays aren't able to sweep people up as they once did. Sure, we are being given a great show of posturing, but humans don't have the stomach for war in the fifth dimension. Kindness and thoughtfulness are starting to prevail and people are starting to think for themselves once again. We can now see more clearly behind ignoble intentions without being duped. The biggest shift, though, is the ability to manifest great, wonderful things with intentions. That is why what I do in shifting people is so effortless and drastic. It is because I am actually just removing the illusions that humans hold as a crutch until they get used to the vibration of the fifth dimension.

Everyone is at a greater state of consciousness than they realize. They are just being shifted slowly so as not to shock their system. It is like easing your toe into the water to get used to the temperature as opposed to diving in. People have brought all their ideas, concepts and even archaic beliefs to the fifth dimension like a security blanket until they feel comfortable giving them up. The thing is, they don't realize it because they have also brought the controlling elements of their comfort items as well.

A client who does the tapping exercises religiously had a dream experience to illustrate what is happening. In the inner worlds, she was driving really fast and efficiently. This represents her ability to accept the freedom of the fifth dimension. Everywhere she drove, she had to zip around all people's belongings that were strewn in the street. (This is their personal baggage they brought with them.) It didn't slow her down, and everyone was pleasant enough, but it did block the streets.

She was then stopped by the police. They accused her of having a weapon. She had a smooth oval object in her hand, but it was not a gun. They tried to arrest her but she argued for her rights. They did confiscate the object though. When she got to the police station to retrieve it, she opened it up and it had essential oils inside. The oval object represented truth. The police were the old engrams of fear and intimidation that were universally established. People hadn't brought only their personal baggage with them to the fifth dimension. They also brought universal concepts that were really limiting. Our old ways of demonizing others are illusions and very tiresome for those of us who have outgrown them. But these universal engrams need to be dissipated by the collective for all to be free.

I had a similar experience of being demonized last night. I was awakened to the authorities asking about me. They used an old name I used to go by and put the word "dead" on the end. There was mass confusion out in the street. People were being released from their old state of consciousness. They were becoming free of third dimension limitations. But it was not presented that way. "Officials" were talking loud and implying that it was a bad accident and it was my fault. No one would charge me or say it to me, but they made a point of having everyone believe I was guilty of causing a horrendous crime. They used innuendos, implications and indirect comments to intimidate.

This plays out in my daily life. As careful and as kind as I can be, watching my thoughts and intentions, I am still disliked by many and demonized in an ethereal way. It is the way it always has been for those who hold the intention of freeing humanity in any subtle way. Many of you may see this happen in your own life. Don't fall for it. Here's to dealing with those old collective engrams and finally eliminating them. They are made of old consciousness, fear and ignoble intentions. It's time to dissipate them so that humanity can enjoy the pristine purity and freedom of the fifth dimension.

(Say each statement three times while tapping on your head and say it a fourth time while tapping on your chest. Then go on to the next.)

"I declare myself a surrogate for the collective in doing these taps; in all moments."

"We strip all denial off of the world in immersing themselves in old engrams; in all moments."

"We release allowing engrams to enslave humanity; in all moments."

"We dissipate the dark psychic energy that uses engrams to enslave the world; in all moments."

"We remove all masks, walls, and armor off engrams; in all moments."

"We expose all power mongers who use engrams to limit humanity; in all moments."

"We release allowing old engrams to exist; in all moments."

"We release allowing old engrams to strip society of its humanity; in all moments."

"We protect all individuals from being swallowed up in old engrams; in all moments."

"We stop old engrams from pimping out humanity; in all moments."

"We stop engrams from lining the pockets of the power mongers; in all moments."

"We stop engrams from seeming legit; in all moments."

"We release allowing old engrams to squelch our freedom; in all moments."

"We release passively watching while engrams flourish in the fifth dimension; in all moments."

"We strip all illusion off of all engrams; in all moments."

"We release being duped by engrams; in all moments."

"We release being separated from our humanity by old engrams; in all moments."

"We release being manipulated by engrams; in all moments."

"We release deferring to engrams; in all moments."

"We release allowing engrams to frame our perception of reality; in all moments."

"We release allowing engrams to shove an agenda down our throat; in all moments."

"We dissolve all engrams of greed and deceit; in all moments."

"We release being kept ignorant to engrams; in all moments."

"We release being duped by engrams; in all moments."

"We release adulating engrams; in all moments."

"We release endorsing engrams; in all moments."

"We release being stripped of our freedom by engrams; in all moments."

"We release having our individuality diminished by engrams; in all moments."

"We release being complacent in perceiving engrams; in all moments."

"We release having our humanity gutted by engrams; in all moments."

"We release being squelched into a hellish existence by engrams; in all moments."

"We eliminate the first cause in the creation or mandating of engrams; in all moments."

"We release all psychic energies of engrams; in all moments."

"We strip all illusion and defenses off those who manipulate using engrams; in all moments."

"We release converting our sacred devotion to Source into deference to engrams; in all moments."

"We release being enslaved to engrams; in all moments."

"We release diminishing ourselves by allowing engrams to exist; in all moments."

"We remove all vivaxes between ourselves and all engrams; in all moments."

"We remove all tentacles between ourselves and all engrams; in all moments."

"We withdraw all our energy from all engrams; in all moments."

"We release being naïve to engrams; in all moments."

"We collapse and dissolve all engrams; in all moments."

"We remove all programming and conditioning that engrams have put on us; in all moments."

"We remove all individual and universal engrams from our whole beingness; in all moments."

"We remove all controlling devices that engrams have put on us; in all moments."

"We release allowing engrams to induce us to fear or hatred; in all moments."

"We release allowing engrams to rob us of our voice, dignity or freedom; in all moments."

"We release the belief that engrams are inevitable; in all moments."

"We send all energy matrices into the light and sound that formulate or enable engrams; in all moments."

"We command all complex energy matrices that formulate or enable engrams be escorted into the light and sound; in all moments."

"We send all energy matrices into the light and sound that make engrams; in all moments."

"We command all complex energy matrices that make up engrams to be escorted into the light and sound; in all moments."

"We send all energy matrices into the light and sound that perpetuate the ignoble intentions of engrams; in all moments."

"We command all complex energy matrices that perpetuate the ignoble intentions of engrams to be escorted into the light and sound; in all moments."

"We release being deceived by engrams; in all moments."

"We nullify all contracts with all engrams; in all moments."

"We recant all vows and agreements between ourselves and all engrams; in all moments."

"We remove all curses between ourselves and all engrams; in all moments."

"We remove all curses that engrams have put on the world; in all moments."

"We remove all blessings between ourselves and all engrams; in all moments."

"We remove all payoffs to perpetrating engrams; in all moments."

"We sever all strings, cords and psychic connection between ourselves and all engrams; in all moments."

"We sever all strings, cords and psychic connection between ourselves all those who support engrams; in all moments."

"We dissipate all psychic streams of energy that allow

engrams to go unchecked; in all moments."

"We dissolve all karmic ties between ourselves and all engrams; in all moments."

"We remove all the pain, burden, limitations, fear, futility unworthiness, anger, abandonment, rejection and illusion of separateness that all engrams have put on us; in all moments."

"We bury all engrams in the weight of their own ignoble intentions; in all moments."

"We paralyze the machine that mandates engrams; in all moments."

"We remove all muscle memory of all engrams; in all moments."

"We break all energy grids between ourselves and all engrams; in all moments."

"We take back all the joy, love, abundance, freedom, health, success, security, companionship, creativity, peace, life, wholeness, beauty, enthusiasm, contentment, spirituality, enlightenment, confidence, ability to discern, individuality and empowerment that all engrams have taken from us; in all moments."

"We disarm the ability of engrams to desecrate humanity; in all moments."

"We disarm the ability of all engrams to enslave

humanity; in all moments."

"We disarm the ability of all engrams to immerse us in lower consciousness; in all moments."

"We strip all engrams of their illusion; in all moments."

"We strip all engrams of their authority; in all moments."

"We disarm all engrams from the ability to dwindle our quality of life; in all moments."

"We eliminate the first cause in engrams tainting civil liberties; in all moments."

"We crumble and dissolve all constructs created by engrams; in all moments."

"We nullify all contracts with the constructs of engrams; in all moments."

"We strip all illusion off those who benefit from engrams; in all moments."

"We eliminate the first cause in all the mandates of engrams; in all moments."

"We hold open all portals for higher consciousness and Universal freedom in all; in all moments."

"We release confusing old engrams with truth; in all moments."

"We release confusing engrams as an inevitable solution; in all moments."

"We release resonating or emanating with old engrams; in all moments."

"We extract all engrams from our individual and Universal Sound Frequency; in all moments."

"We extract all engrams from our individual and Universal Light Emanation; in all moments."

"We extract all engrams from all 32 layers of our individual and Universal aura; in all moments."

"We extract all engrams from our whole beingness; in all moments."

"We blast pure divine love into all aspects of the world that engrams have tainted; in all moments."

"We shift our paradigm from engrams to the higher consciousness of individual and universal Joy, Love, Abundance, Freedom, Health, Peace, Strength, Empowerment and Integrity; in all moments."

"We transcend engrams; in all moments."

"We make space in the world for Universal Higher consciousness; in all moments."

"We remove all blockages to Universal Higher consciousness; in all moments."

"We stretch our capacity to fathom and embrace Universal higher consciousness; in all moments."

"We are centered and empowered in the higher consciousness of Universal Peace and Freedom; in all moments."

"We infuse the higher consciousness of Universal Peace and Freedom into our Sound frequency; in all moments."

"We imbue the higher consciousness of Universal Peace and Freedom into our Light Emanation; in all moments."

"We resonate, emanate and are interconnected to all life in the higher consciousness of Universal Peace and Freedom; in all moments."

As I finish writing this, I become physically ill and dizzy. I have to run to the bathroom and lie down after they are shared. If it were easy to break through all the resistance to higher consciousness, we would all be enjoying a more evolved state and be free of illness and despair. Please break through the resistance to doing this exercise. The payoff for humanity and earth is immeasurable.

17: DEALING WITH TROLLS IN LIFE

On social media, the trolls are negative people that look for places to dump negativity and bring doubt to truth. They may be masked under the guise of interesting stories or truth, but they provide a false and destructive narrative. If you think about it, we have been dealing with those kinds of interferences in our everyday life as well:

- People who gossip or make up negative stories merely to get attention
- People who complain
- Those who mock others and are bullies
- People who profess gloom
- Those who mandate laws for personal gain.

None of these people are really dealing with truth because truth is an expansion of consciousness.

- Truth creates a break in the gloomy clouds of conjecture.
- Truth is not a bantering of opinions.
- Truth is not a titillating discussion slanted to personal bias.

- Truth is not rhetoric or false narrative.
- Truth is not a consensus of popular opinion.
- Truth is subjective from your vantage point, like the sun being in different positions depending where you are in the world.
- But truth, like the sun, is unwavering.

When I write something of truth, you can tell people's vantage point to truth by how vehemently they attack. It is like someone who is immersed in low-level clouds of a valley resenting that others can feel the warmth of the rays of sun on their face. Instead of trying to see through a break in the clouds, they will attack the position of the sun. They attack truth.

Dogma and ritual still have a place in people's lives. People enjoy the social aspect of praising a God they can't see but they imagine wants to be adored. But they may be ignoring the nature of God. People who use God to mandate laws to diminish others are committing blasphemy. Anyone who lacks compassion is committing blasphemy. Anyone who mocks, scorns, belittles or cheats other beings is committing blasphemy. Anyone who destroys the pristine nature of the earth that provides all life is committing blasphemy.

The laws of man are running directly OPPOSITE the nature of God with such a haughty, ugly flare that all who use a pious bias SHOULD be escorted into a hell of their own design. It would be a hell that they have mandated for other beings. Perhaps that is what karma is: getting what you thrust upon others.

It is enough for people to see the truth of these blasphemies and use their intentions to dissipate their ability to affect others. Shame on those who allow such atrocities to be mandated without acknowledging their part in perpetuating them. Sometimes it is scary to write truth because of all the lifetimes I have been killed for speaking up and advocating for truth.

But what is scarier is living amongst a world of people who sit by complacently and don't share their gifts or involve themselves into delving into truth because it is too awkward or uncomfortable. It is appalling to see the complacency, indifference and apathy in man while others suffer so atrociously. Apathy and indifference to truth are scarier than any disease man can invent to contaminate his fellow man. Please do what you can to fight the plague of it.

18: HAVE YOU BEEN FEELING THE UPGRADES?

I now realize what the upgrades that I have been feeling for humans are. All the organs are being detoxed and upgraded. We are moving totally off the linear grid and there is no aging, disease or decay in exponential existence. But the upgrades are acclimating to our belief system.

Children born now are not so trapped in linear limitations and they readily accept upgrades. If you think about it, aging, disease and decay are all accumulative things. There is no accumulating on a starburst because it is perpetually expanding outward. The concept of stagnant energy, which all health issues are, is dissipated.

All of humanity was detoxed of its insanity and issues. People are freer to awaken. People with mental illness aren't defective. They are just not adhering to the linear rules put on them. They are freer. We are all freer to be exponential.

In our old belief system, we consciously outflow

through giving of ourselves or staying busy. This is most like exponential energy while being in a linear existence. It is our compromise. But beings are being born just to be outflow and not have to fight the limitations of a linear "current." What we are experiencing now is teaching us to relax and not need to try to outflow so hard.

Our energy naturally outflows when the brain does not confine it to a linear perimeter. This is the upgrade that we are experiencing in the intense detox or change in sleep patterns. A starburst doesn't need as much sleep. But a starburst submerged in linear limitations may need more sleep to learn how to emerge from the linear limitations.

I hope this helps.

19: ELIMINATE DARK MONEY

They say the love of money is the root of all evil. Dark money is the means for evil to entrench itself in the governing of good people. Men can look shiny and positive enough. They can hide behind passages of the Bible and love of country. But they are using the most sacred texts and ideals of the people to rape those same people of their freedom, to rob the land of its essence and to manipulate greedy, selfish people into doing their will.

Innocents are at the mercy at the bombardment of their psyche by those wielding dark money. Those who live simple lives and have simple desires to care for their families have no reference point for such ignoble agendas. They can hardly conceptualize such dastardly deeds, let alone see behind the façade intricately manufactured by evildoers to look wholesome, while gutting the earth of all that is sacred and organic.

(Say each statement three times while tapping on your head and say it a fourth time while tapping on your chest. Then go on to the next.)

"I declare myself a surrogate for humanity in doing these taps; in all moments."

"We strip all denial off of the world in dealing with dark money; in all moments."

"We release allowing dark money to buy up the earth; in all moments."

"We dissipate the systemic indifference that allows dark money to limit the quality of life for all; in all moments."

"We remove all masks, walls, and armor off of the use of dark money; in all moments."

"We remove all masks, walls, and armor off of using dark money to elect unqualified officials; in all moments."

"We release allowing dark money to strip individuals' civil liberties; in all moments."

"We prevent dark money from wielding personal power; in all moments."

"We prevent dark money from wielding power for big business; in all moments."

"We release allowing dark money to diminish our freedom of choice; in all moments."

"We release passively watching while big business buys

and sells elected public officials using dark money; in all moments."

"We strip all illusion off of dark money; in all moments."

"We release being indifferent or apathetic in the use of dark money; in all moments."

"We release being separated from our humanity by dark money; in all moments."

"We release being manipulated by dark money; in all moments."

"We release dark money framing society's conception of God; in all moments."

"We break up the cluster of power mongers that use dark money to cheat people; in all moments."

"We release being pulled back into ignorance by dark money; in all moments."

"We release being enamored with dark money in all moments."

"We release being stripped of our progressiveness by dark money; in all moments."

"We release being complacent with the use of dark money; in all moments."

"We release having our humanity gutted by dark

money; in all moments."

"We release the worship of dark money; in all moments."

"We eliminate the first cause in the creation and use of dark money; in all moments."

"We release being deceived by dark money; in all moments."

"We strip all illusion and defenses off those who use dark money to control others; in all moments."

"We release converting our sacred devotion to God into worship of dark money; in all moments."

"We release being enslaved to dark money; in all moments."

"We release diminishing ourselves by allowing dark money to mandate civil liberties; in all moments."

"We remove all vivaxes between ourselves and dark money; in all moments."

"We remove all tentacles between ourselves and dark money; in all moments."

"We withdraw all our energy from dark money; in all moments."

"We collapse and dissolve all opportunities to wield dark money; in all moments."

"We remove all programming and conditioning that dark money has put on us; in all moments."

"We remove all individual and universal engrams of dark money; in all moments."

"We release worshipping dark money; in all moments."

"We release allowing dark money to rob us of our voice; in all moments."

"We release the belief that the use of dark money is inevitable; in all moments."

"We send all energy matrices into the light and sound that enable dark money; in all moments."

"We command all complex energy matrices that enable dark money to be escorted into the light and sound; in all moments."

"We send all energy matrices into the light and sound that worship dark money; in all moments."

"We command all complex energy matrices that worship dark money to be escorted into the light and sound; in all moments."

"We send all energy matrices into the light and sound that prevent us from eliminating dark money; in all moments."

"We command all complex energy matrices that

prevent us from eliminating dark money to be escorted into the light and sound; in all moments."

"We release being deceived by dark money; in all moments."

"We recant all vows and agreements between ourselves and dark money; in all moments."

"We remove all curses between ourselves and all dark money; in all moments."

"We remove all blessings between ourselves dark money; in all moments."

"We remove all payoffs to all those who use dark money; in all moments."

"We sever all strings, cords and psychic connection between ourselves and all dark money; in all moments."

"We dissipate all psychic streams of energy that perpetuate dark money; in all moments."

"We dissolve all karmic ties between ourselves and all dark money; in all moments."

"We remove all the pain, burden, limitations, fear, futility, unworthiness and illusion of separateness that dark money has put on us; in all moments."

"We bury dark money in the weight of its own ignoble intentions; in all moments."

"We remove all muscle memory that causes us to defer to dark money; in all moments."

"We dismantle all energy grids between ourselves and dark money; in all moments."

"We take back all the joy, love, abundance, freedom, health, success, security, companionship, creativity, peace, life, wholeness, beauty, enthusiasm, contentment, spirituality, enlightenment, confidence, ability to discern, and empowerment that dark money has taken from us; in all moments."

"We strip the ability of dark money to deceive; in all moments."

"We strip dark money of its illusion of propriety; in all moments."

"We disarm dark money from the ability to take away our civil liberties; in all moments."

"We crumble and dissolve all constructs created by dark money; in all moments."

"We nullify all contracts with dark money; in all moments."

"We strip all illusion off those who benefit from using dark money; in all moments."

"We eliminate the first cause in all mandates of dark money; in all moments."

"We hold open a portal for Universal integrity in all; in all moments."

"We release confusing dark money with anything of integrity; in all moments."

"We release confusing dark money with greatness; in all moments."

"We release resonating or emanating with dark money; in all moments."

"We extract all dark money from our individual and Universal Sound Frequency; in all moments."

"We extract all dark money from our individual and Universal Light Emanation; in all moments."

"We extract all dark money from all 32 layers of our individual and Universal aura; in all moments."

"We extract all of dark money from our whole beingness; in all moments."

"We shift our paradigm from dark money to individual and Universal Joy, Love, Abundance, Freedom, Health, Peace, Strength, and Empowerment; in all moments."

"We transcend dark money; in all moments."

"We are centered and empowered in integrity; in all moments."

"We infuse integrity into our Sound frequency; in all

moments."

"We imbue integrity into our Light Emanation; in all moments."

"We resonate, emanate and are interconnected to all life integrity; in all moments."

20: MOVING FROM LINEAR TO EXPONENTIAL

This is information the Ancient Ones told me because I was still upset that Bernie was not the next president. They reminded me of what they have been explaining to me about the world going from a male centered world to an exponential reality. Male energy, through its domination, has been thwarting the natural process of evolution way too long.

Those with vested interests have been buying up technology that would eliminate our enslavement to fossil fuels and Western medicine and putting it on the shelf. These are both big money makers for the top one-percent. But this interruption in the evolution of the planet is not going to be allowed to continue. We, as a species, are in the process of even transcending beyond the illusion of monetary gluttony. It is a synthetic form of abundance that we all have been conditioned to buy into. Even this will fall away.

We are moving from a linear existence that constricts all of humanity to being stick figures. It is an existence where all creativity, inspiration, diversity and genius are thwarted at every turn. It is the nightmare that we are experiencing now where the only ingenuity comes, when someone so frustrated with the current standards, can only stand out as special by blowing themselves to bits or gunning down others in the streets.

We are all experiencing the horrific reality that comes from such systemic apathy and disdain. No, this is not how such dynamic beings were meant to live. We are moving away from a mentality that is totally about winning at all costs and pits all species and people against each other to survive. It is such a ruthless hierarchy that puts humans at the top and then compartmentalizes them even further by sect, sex and skin color. How barbaric is that?

We are moving away from a linear existence of such limiting impingement on freedom, that only the movement from birth to death is celebrated in how we measure up in comparison to others. Those who deviate from the norm in any way are demonized and persecuted. Until now, it truly has been the "human race" because we have all been in a competition with each other to be considered the best at being normal.

But all this is changing. We are moving towards an exponential existence that is no longer dominated by male energy. The innate qualities of female energy are going to be mingled with what we are already experiencing. Male energy, without female energy, shows up as a brute mentality. It is eager to win at all costs and to be superior in the ranking system.

Female energy is responsible for our compassion, empathy and the use of our subtle senses of intuition and natural healing. So many of us individuals have evolved to outgrow the thirst for winning at all costs, fear mongering or diminishing others to better ourselves. Where male energy is driven to win at all costs, female energy is all about a sisterhood where every scenario is a win-win.

This is the Universal balance that we are being catapulted to. Those who have gained privilege in a male dominated society, those of affluence and the preferred color skin, are fearful to give up their edge. This is what we are seeing play out in the world to no avail. The evolution of humanity is bigger than the temper tantrums of the "upper class."

So the political system of the future is not going to be as much of a hierarchy. The person at the top position is going to mean less and less as individuals take back their empowerment. The positions, as they stand, will be more like props for the people to get used to the shift of empowerment back to themselves. Because Hillary is a woman, I was able to tap into the energy that was being generated and poured into her. All the energy of money, greed and power that was going to her, I was able to draw through her and return it to the earth. I actually was very attentive to the entire speech that she gave. Not to her, but to this process.

As Hillary accepted the nomination for president, I did some powerful energy work. I was told that female makeup is different. That it is difficult for female energy to hold the reigns of male energy because the world has been distorted to a male preference. As ruthless as she and her husband are, she would not be able to hold the large stockpile of power that was poured into her by the most affluent power mongers on the planet. In fact, the only reason that she was able to gain such abilities was by drawing on her husband's tried and true ruthless ways of maintaining power at all costs. But in her hands alone, it would be a shaky commodity. Her having all that power at her hands at that moment was when the Ancient Ones caused me to act.

It was because she is a woman and I am female energy personified that I could tap into all that energy she had accumulated, pass it through her, through myself and pour it back where it rightfully belongs: into the trees and directly into the earth. It is the earth's energy that has been raped and hoarded, so I gave it back to its rightful owner. This whole scenario that was playing out for the sake of the evolution of humanity was all preordained. She was playing her part and I was playing mine.

I was told that the purpose of her getting to that

position with all the power was simply so all the misappropriated energy could be given back to the earth and put back into play by all. I have been preparing all my lifetimes to know what to do in that moment. As I was drawing energy through the "wand" of Hillary and pouring it back into the earth, I wondered if people would be angry with me. But then I was told that this is what the people who really care want to have done with it. It was everyone's inheritance. It was not just viable to a few. I was performing a service for humanity itself. It was a very profound moment.

I think that this was the purpose of her getting this far was about. I have been doing very active energy work to starve out power and greed in the world. I know it sounds naive to some, but those who know me and know what I do may appreciate that this is possible. I am not done in returning all that has been depleted from the earth. But now it is in a better position to nurture and replenish itself again. It is our responsibility to nurture it in return with gratitude and kindness to all. Just saying.

We will see a renaissance of individuals coming forth in a variant of talents and genius pouring higher consciousness into the wrench of the status quo. World peace was never meant to look like socialism. World peace is about an explosion of creativity and purpose that can't distract individuals from doing anything but what they love.

Bernie is instrumental in this happening. He would be distracted as president by the attacks against him coming from opposition. But as someone who receives more respect and is seen as having more passion and integrity than the other two combined, Bernie is in a better position to move the government system to an exponential reality.

It may be a blow to our egos but if this is the price we pay for such an upgrade, so be it. Greatness always causes great suffering to the ego. It is part of the formula. Ask any great soul who has come here to serve. Bernie's vision of a revolution and everyone rising up was accurate. It just doesn't feel accurate because he is explaining something that is happening exponentially and putting it into the confines of physical terms.

Bernie is also right that it is irrelevant that he be president. He will still be playing his part in history.

It is happening. I can assure you. It is the vision that John Lennon viewed and was inspired by. One day in contemplation, I was seeing an empowered world. As I was looking onto such a world, I saw John Lennon looking on as well. It was like two people sitting on a hill in silence aware of the other but in an oblique way.

If you are able to tune in to the more subtle realms, use

this post as a road map to see the reality that John and I witnessed. The more people who can tap into this vision, the "more quickly" it can be realized. We all do our part. It does not have to be done in a demonstrative way. What we believe and cherish in the sanctity of our own realms does matter. In your quiet assertions of Joy, Love, Abundance and Freedom for all, you are manifesting a better reality for us all.

21: FREE HUMANITY OF ALL DRUGS, OPIOIDS AND ADDICTIONS

It is obvious that the issues with drugs, opioids and addictions are entrenched with our psyche. They need to be addressed on a deeper level to eliminate them. Ignoring who we are as energy beings keeps us trapped in the vice of drug use and addiction. In more naïve times, drug use was associated with our spiritual seeking. For some, it has been a past life memory of taking a spiritual quest with such herbs as ayawaska. But we no longer have this luxury. Even those sweet memories will be used to entrench the individual into a web of nightmares as a means to spread malice. We are all so much wiser now.

Because psychic savvy greedy whores will use our most sacred quests to lure us into their trademarked version of hell, the innocent, naïve and those seeking spiritual adventure run the risk of being trapped in such states.
 A few years ago, I advised a younger client on the use of drugs and to abstain from them when seeking spiritual attainment. She respected me in all ways

except this one. She argued that the youth associated drug use with spirituality. This same woman is the one who reached out for assistance in helping relieve the systemic abuse of drugs in the world today. People her age are now dying horrific deaths.

What we need to realize is that we are no longer rogues on the road of life. We are exponential beings that access the collective group of beings with our intentions and motivations. When one submits to doing drugs, even if it is harmless to them, they are opening the door of all humanity to accept them a little more. It is like giving permission to all those who would otherwise have the inclination to abstain. Whenever you agree to anything, realize what you are agreeing to. You may be on the one polar opposite side of an issue. You may be filled with noble, spiritual intentions. But as soon as you agree to something, you are connected to the whole of that something, even the opposition.

If you understand this principle and still choose to allow space in the world for drug use through your own agreement, you are holding space for the destructive psychic energies to take root in this physical world. The same is true with any form of abuse. It is not always the case in a fair and just world. But these psychic energies of power, greed and destruction have been inundating our world and have gone unchecked until now. We no longer can afford our naïve and passive state. Everyone must grow an energetic pair, forgo the indulgence of passivity and acknowledge themselves as the energetic beings that they are.

People are waiting for God to save them. Yet every time God sends truth, people scoff, ignore or ridicule it. That is on them. It is now on all of humanity. If you are grateful for God's guidance, you will stop arguing over the substance and the sex of Source and accept the help where it is given. These exercises of you tapping are you acknowledging your empowerment and using your talents as an energetic being to return the world to a balance. It does not matter if you understand your own gifts; trust the process of realizing them. This is what this tapping exercise can afford you and humanity.

By agreeing to them, you are agreeing to your own empowerment. You are agreeing to the power of a good intention and a noble cause. You are transcending. Doing these taps is writing your name in your own book of Revelations.

(Say each statement three times while tapping on your head and say it a fourth time while tapping on your chest.)

"I declare myself a surrogate for humanity in doing these taps; in all moments."

"We gift all those with addictions the strength to transcend them; in all moments."

"We strip all denial off of the world in dealing with drugs, opioids and addictions; in all moments."

"We release allowing drugs and addictions to run the world; in all moments."

"We dissipate the systemic indifference that allows drugs, opioids and addictions to flourish; in all moments."

"We remove all masks, walls and armor off of all drugs, opioids and addictions; in all moments."

"We release the burden of being saddled with drugs, opioids and addictions; in all moments."

"We release allowing drugs, opioids and addictions to take our children; in all moments."

"We release allowing drugs, opioids and addictions to diminish our quality of life; in all moments."

"We release passively watching while drugs, opioids and addictions hold the world hostage; in all moments."

"We strip all illusion off of drugs, opioids and addictions; in all moments."

"We release allowing drugs, opioids and addictions to pull us into their psychic grip; in all moments."

"We release being indifferent, or apathetic to drugs, opioids and addictions; in all moments."

"We release being separated from our humanity by drugs, opioids and addictions; in all moments."

"We release being manipulated by drugs, opioids and addictions; in all moments."

"We break up the cluster of power mongers that use drugs, opioids and addictions to reign; in all moments."

"We release being plummeted into ignorance by drugs, opioids and addictions; in all moments."

"We release enabling drugs, opioids and addictions; in all moments."

"We release being stripped of our progressiveness by drugs, opioids and addictions; in all moments."

"We release being complacent with drugs, opioids and addictions; in all moments."

"We release ever empowering drugs, opioids and addictions in any way; in all moments."

"We eliminate the first cause in the creation of drugs, opioids and addictions; in all moments."

"We release being enamored with drugs, opioids and addictions; in all moments."

"We strip all illusion and defenses off those who perpetuate drugs, opioids and addictions to control others; in all moments."

"We release converting our empowerment to complacency of drugs, opioids and addictions; in all moments."

"We release being enslaved to drugs, opioids and addictions; in all moments."

"We release diminishing ourselves by using drugs, opioids and addictions; in all moments."

"We remove all vivaxes between ourselves and drugs, opioids and addictions; in all moments."

"We remove all tentacles between ourselves and drugs, opioids and addictions; in all moments."

"We withdraw all our energy from all drugs, opioids and addictions; in all moments."

"We collapse and dissolve all portals to drugs, opioids and addictions; in all moments."

"We remove all programming and conditioning that drugs, opioids and addictions have put on us; in all moments."

"We remove all individual and universal engrams of drugs, opioids and addictions; in all moments."

"We release worshipping drugs, opioids and addictions; in all moments."

"We release allowing drugs, opioids and addictions to

rob us of our voice; in all moments."

"We release feeding drugs, opioids and addictions with adulation or fear; in all moments."

"We send all energy matrices into the light and sound that enable drugs, opioids and addictions; in all moments."

"We command all complex energy matrices that enable drugs, opioids and addictions to be escorted into the light and sound; in all moments."

"We send all energy matrices into the light and sound that allow drugs, opioids and addictions to grip individuals; in all moments."

"We command all complex energy matrices that allow drugs, opioids and addictions to grip individuals to be escorted into the light and sound; in all moments."

"We send all energy matrices into the light and sound that prevent us from eliminating drugs, opioids and addictions; in all moments."

"We command all complex energy matrices that prevent us from eliminating drugs, opioids and addictions to be escorted into the light and sound; in all moments."

"We recant all vows and agreements between ourselves and drugs, opioids and addictions; in all moments."

"We remove all curses between ourselves and all drugs, opioids and addictions; in all moments."

"We remove all blessings between ourselves and all drugs, opioids and addictions; in all moments."

"We remove the perceived payoff of using drugs, opioids, and addictions; in all moments."

"We sever all strings, cords and psychic connection between ourselves and all drugs, opioids and addictions; in all moments."

"We dissolve all karmic ties between ourselves and all drugs, opioids and addictions; in all moments."

"We remove all the pain, burden, limitations, fear, futility, unworthiness, and illusion of separateness that drugs, opioids and addictions have put on us; in all moments."

"We bury drugs, opioids and addictions in their own ignoble intentions; in all moments."

"We remove all muscle memory that causes us to defer to drugs, opioids and addictions; in all moments."

"We dismantle all energy grids between ourselves and all drugs, opioids and addictions; in all moments."

"We take back all the joy, love, abundance, freedom, health, success, security, companionship, creativity, peace, life, wholeness, beauty, enthusiasm, contentment, spirituality, enlightenment, confidence, ability to discern and empowerment that drugs, opioids and addictions have taken from us; in all moments."

"We strip drugs, opioids and addictions of their girth; in all moments."

"We strip drugs, opioids and addictions of their illusions of grandeur; in all moments."

"We disarm drugs, opioids and addictions from manipulating our children; in all moments."

"We crumble all constructs created by drugs, opioids and addictions; in all moments."

"We nullify all contracts with all drugs, opioids and addictions; in all moments."

"We strip all illusion off of all mandates of drugs, opioids and addictions; in all moments."

"We eliminate the first cause in all mandates of drugs, opioids and addictions; in all moments."

"We hold an open portal for universal strength, freedom and empowerment of individuals; in all moments."

"We release confusing drugs, opioids and addictions with a rite of passage; in all moments."

"We release confusing drugs, opioids and addictions

with salvation; in all moments."

"We release resonating or emanating with drugs, opioids and addictions; in all moments."

"We extract all of drugs, opioids and addictions from our individual and Universal Sound Frequency; in all moments."

"We extract all of drugs, opioids and addictions from our individual and Universal Light Emanation; in all moments."

"We extract all of drugs, opioids and addictions from all 32 layers of our individual and Universal aura; in all moments."

"We extract all of drugs, opioids and addictions from our whole beingness; in all moments."

"We shift our paradigm from drugs, opioids and addictions to individual and universal Joy, Love, Abundance, Freedom, Health, Peace, Strength and Empowerment; in all moments."

"We transcend drugs, opioids and addictions; in all moments."

"We are centered and empowered in individual and Universal Joy, Love, Abundance, Freedom, Health, Peace, Strength and Empowerment; in all moments."

"We infuse individual and Universal Joy, Love,

Abundance, Freedom, Health, Peace, Strength and Empowerment into our sound frequency; in all moments."

"We imbue individual and Universal Joy, Love, Abundance, Freedom, Health, Peace, Strength and Empowerment into our light emanation; in all moments."

"We resonate, emanate and are interconnected to all life in individual and Universal Joy, Love, Abundance, Freedom, Health, Peace, Strength and Empowerment; in all moments."

22: WHAT AWARE SOULS DO

Energy matches the vibration of the things it clings to just like dew clings to a morning leaf. That dew could believe it is a part of the leaf. That is what it "knows" as its identity. In the same way, the energies that collect within an area can take on personal characteristics.

A house is full of all your thoughts, emotions and habitual interactions bouncing around and permeating the atmosphere. There is no need to sensationalize it or give it further life by being fearful of it. It is merely a condensation and collection of human interactions identifying with those actions and thus developing a persona.

Fear and inactivity are great ways to coagulate the energy. Inactivity slows down the natural flow of energy. Just as pure water will stagnate if it is left standing still, so will energy. Most issues in the body will clear up if you simply remove the fear and move fresh energy into it. This is why people with open minds and open hearts in general are healthier. Their energy, as it is implied by the word "open," is more fluid so they do not collect stagnant energy in the body as easily.

Complaining, gossiping, judging, and labeling are all ways of coagulating the energy. Regret stops the movement of energy cold. Kindness, acceptance, non-reactionary state and gratitude are means of keeping the energy flowing. Put an open-minded person next to a bigoted one, and you can see the difference in how stagnant energy pinches the features and the intellect of the bigot. The open-minded person's features and energy will remain more round and open. Stagnant energy ages a person.

Western medicine is big on labeling issues. This is a means of coagulating the energy further so it has actual mass and weight. When an issue has mass and weight, it is a validation for Western medicine. Western medicine is based on this validation. Of course, your mind being a 3D printer can produce anything you program it to, even disease.

Alternative medicine deals more obliquely with issues. Energy workers see the issue for what it is--blocked and stagnant energy. They don't use the blockage as validation for their work. They use the absence of blockages to validate it. That is why people who are more immersed in materialism gravitate to Western medicine. People who don't need such validation remain healthier.

Many people need their results to be concrete evidence because they have lost the ability to perceive in energy. They are flying blind in this way and cling to the most validating means of reacting. Unfortunately, this includes burning or cutting away at their beautiful body at the site of the clogged energy instead of merely figuring out what is causing the blockage and releasing it.

Alternative medicine is an oxymoron because it is the one most natural and conducive to wellness. Our body deals with releasing stagnant energy on a regular basis. It is a natural process that happens literally as naturally as breathing. As you inhale, your body breath is scanning the body for blockages. As you exhale, it is releasing and repairing them.

Our body deals with these blockages on a regular basis. If left alone, the body will remove these blockages naturally before a person has an inclination to put a label on them. But once a diagnosis is involved, the conscious mind gets involved with fear, dread, and mocking up worst case scenarios. Once this happens, it coagulates the issue even more so and is more difficult to remove. This is why Western medicine preaches early detection. Its validation depends on the conscious mind getting involved and coagulating the energy further to create a more solid diagnosis.

When the body gets overwhelmed with issues, it will

store them in the diaphragm to release later when the body is in a more relaxed state. If it can't get to them in due time, it will bubble wrap them in a fat cell and store them in the body to release later.

That is why losing weight is so difficult for some. It isn't merely about decreasing intake of food. It is about creating a more fluid atmosphere for energy to move around the body while unpacking all the emotional issues it has packed in fat cells. When losing weight, you are dealing with all the emotional issues that were once stored. You are unpacking them to release. That is why people are so moody when dieting. But if they become more active, it is a way of processing these issues more readily.

Being healthy in general entails keeping your energy as fluid as possible. If you think about the past too much, it creates a stoppage of your emotional energy. If you worry about the future too much it creates a stoppage of your mental energy. If you are too sedentary, it causes you to regret the moment and revert to either the past or present too easily. Physical, emotional, and mental energy are important to keep fluid.

That is another reason personal beliefs need to change as well as physical and emotional points to be optimally healthy. Beliefs cause a collecting point for stagnant energy in the body. Everything else in the body could be moving at a great pace, but these beliefs that may be so ingrained might be markers in our energy system that can cause a literal sticking point in our health.

Things like religious limitations, genetic markers and emotional attachments to ethnicity or opinions are a great way to clog energy. It's like posting a stick in pure fluid water. It will collect moss to it over time. These rigid belief systems are like moss collectors in our energy field. If you want to know how a person becomes less fluid as an energy system, look at their beliefs.

The great thing about this understanding is that one can just free up their energy system by having an understanding of it as fluid energy. One limitation even open-minded people put on it is looking at it as two-dimensional. Those who use visualizations imagine energy coming into the top of the head and moving through the body. Even this is a limited belief system.

Energy is coming into us from all angles and all directions. It is more realistic to envision oneself as a car going through a car wash and being permeated with water jets from all sides. Energy flows in from all directions and emanates out from us in all directions. We are more like a starburst in space than a stick figure moving through life as if we are on a conveyor belt of time.

We are expansive, dynamic, multidimensional,

expressive beings. The more we see ourselves this way, the more we can maintain a dynamic center that is not on any manmade linear timeline. We are sovereign beings. As sovereign beings we have no need to subjugate or diminish any other beings. This would cause them to be "clingy" to our energy field. No. We understand to maintain a totally free orbit we must allot this freedom to all others, so they will not inadvertently impinge our freedom by bumping into our orbit. This is what aware souls do.

23: THE QUICKEST ROUTE TO TRANSCENDENCE

Water takes different forms. So does consciousness. In a way, they are similar. In water, there is solid (ice), liquid and gas (air). It is really important for water to stay fluid to maintain its purity. If it sits too long, it becomes stagnant and must be dumped into the ground to be purified through passing through the soil and recollecting itself into a running stream.

All of this is similar to the human consciousness. Some individual molecules of human consciousness are very rigid in their belief system. They live a fear-based life. They are like ice. Most are a mixture of fear and love so they function well enough but still have their limitations. They are in the "water" stage.

Some people are looking around and realizing all the limitations that have been put on them. They are starting to discern truth for themselves. They are looking around and questioning all the conditioning that has been put on us and realize that they have not really been born into a truthful reality. These people have started the evaporation process.

The evaporation process is when water moves from liquid to gas. In the human consciousness, the evaporation process is referred to as awakening, enlightenment or transcendence. As a species, we are in the process of evaporating. We will still have the same properties of "water." We will still have awareness of ourselves and all the positive aspects of being "water." We will just have more spaciousness to live, breathe, think, emote, love and be joyful than ever before.

When all of humanity is in this state, we will have transcended together. It is a scary process for many because they have an understanding of life based on the lies believed by "ice" people. One cannot be ice and air at the same time. Individual atoms may evaporate which is what happens when we drop the physical form. But for the whole state of the world to change, all the properties of ice must be dissipated.

Anger, manipulation, greed, bigotry, selfishness are all aspects of the ice people. The bond that holds the ice molecules together in society is fear. It is glue, a very strong bonding glue. Some people enjoy being ice. They enjoy the power and security of it. There is fear in being water and that fear keeps them in ice form.

They love being ice so much that they administer fear to others merely to have company in the ice state. Ice isn't ice unless there is more than one molecule of it. It takes a lot of fear these days to keep people bonding in ice. It is a hard state to keep forcing onto others. So those who love ice and are good at it have introduced lies to everyone.

They tell them they must behave a certain way, believe a certain thing or worship a certain way, or there will be negative consequences. They know that fear is a way to keep people in ice consciousness. Instead of always needing to work to keep them in a state of fear, they introduce the beliefs that will cause the individuals to keep themselves in a state of fear. It is effortless. They up the stakes on all the individuals and make them fearful of others. That way they will work to keep not only themselves in a state of fear, they will keep their neighboring molecules glued in fear as well.

These ice-loving individuals figured out that love made people more fluid. They knew love dissipated the fear. They had to really trick people into staying ice. So they took the most pure concept they could imagine, which was the creator of all, and gave it qualities to induce fear. Since the real Source was loving and kind, they could not allow people to gravitate to it because that would transform them into water and perhaps even help them evaporate consciously into air.

So they conditioned all individuals, through painful indoctrination, to see the benevolent creator as a ruthless overlord, someone who inflicted pain and punishment. They called him God. Man did ruthless, horrible things to others and said it was the will of God. These people so wanted to stay in the ice consciousness that they created the total opposite attributes of Source and had man worship the opposite of Source. This ensured that they would never transcend.

Another thing they did to immerse individuals in fear was to introduce the concept of death. They confused the beautiful experience of evaporation or transcendence with something that they conjured as horrific and final. They made people believe that the temporary shift in consciousness of one lifetime was the finality of it all. They halted their understanding of experiencing many lifetimes of evaporating and becoming condensation again and again.

They instilled this belief system as an outer mandate. If someone felt the innate sense of truth, wonder and expression within themselves, the other individuals would turn on them. They would demonize and stigmatize them. They were burned at the stake as witches, shunned from society, labeled tree huggers, hippies, flakes. All the while preventing the truth, love and expansiveness of consciousness that these individuals were experiencing from melting the ice. This torturing of advanced souls became so systemic that the mere thought of transcending induced individuals into fear. This was a perfect way to keep everyone as ice.

The problem that those who love the security of being ice find is that there are too many individuals veering towards transcending. It is not enough to demonize individuals anymore. To stay as ice, there needs to be a mass agreement that these individuals are evil. The ice lovers must introduce even more fear to the mix to prevent themselves from transcending. So they make an enemy out of all those who are gearing towards transcendence.

They give them a label to be able to identify them clearly. They call them left wing. They deem them the enemy. They could be our children, parents, or friends. But they still become the enemy that is trying to destroy us when, in actuality, the love that we experience is the conduit that keeps us all connected as water. They are not our enemy. They are an aspect of all of us. They are us in another form with a different set of conditions that affords them a different vantage point. We are all one component.

When water does not flow though, it becomes stagnant. If the ice lovers can't keep us all in the consciousness of ice, they will do the next best thing. They will have us turn on ourselves as enemies and prevent our fluid movement within ourselves. This is what we are seeing with trying to prevent individuals from migrating around the world. The walls we build enforce a stagnant state of consciousness. Creating a stagnant state of consciousness is the next best thing to being ice to those who prefer to be ice. They strive to keep us immersed in a state of apathy.

A way to prevent this is for those who are love based to continue to be love based. The ice lovers WANT everyone to turn away from love and stay immersed in fighting. That is considered a win for them. They will do everything they can to keep humanity immersed in negativity and fear at all costs. That is the only way they prevent the natural evolution of transcendence that is happening.

If they can turn peace lovers back into fear mongers, they have been effective. That is why raising awareness on horrific issues can be counterproductive. If we all raise our awareness to love, peace and truth, we will be more effective than taking on an individual plight. Many times, those who do this are doing the work of those who want to stay ice.

To counter this, if you are love based, continue to be love based. If there are those who limit themselves and others, have compassion for them because you were once at that phase too. Encourage them with loving intentions. You were once the most despicable you could be as well. It is a fantastic way to learn power. You abused power once. Now you suffer with those memories. It drives the need to do anything you can to not ever abuse power again.

Let the lowest common denominators of the world learn their lessons quickly and thoroughly. Have compassion for the anguish they inflict on themselves. Dissipate their fear with your love. Encourage them inwardly that they will be fine and all fear is a temporary state. They are praying for guidance from a vengeful man made God. May they be answered by a truthful, loving expression of Source. Be the molecule of God that answers them. It is the quickest, most efficient route to transcendence.

24: DISSIPATING MORE PSYCHIC STREAMS OF ENERGY

A LIFEBOAT TO WORLD PEACE

Think about the people trapped in a society of a dictator. I wonder if they are awakening too. They are cut off from a healthy understanding of other cultures and think of everyone as the enemy. In quiet times, I feed truth into the cultures that don't have access to anything but adulating their leader.

I don't give it to them in words. That would be putting my spin on it. What I do is see the grayness of their existence in panoramic view and brush stroke it with my awareness, love and gratitude. It is a way to bring them up to speed and to crumble the prison that is induced onto them.

Because the only real weapon that a dictator has over his people is their own ignorance and fear coupled with the fear he induces. This is a formula for psychic control. That is really all that is happening in dictator dynamics. It is that a larger than life character induces the people into feeding him their energy with very real threats.

He then uses their energy to seem even larger than life to take more and more energy from his people. Before they realize that the dictator is ruthless or unethical, it is too late to effectively break the stronghold that has been set in motion energetically. The key is to dissipate the psychic energies that are holding people in this dynamic. Dissipate it with an understanding of the process because awareness is the fix.

It happens in any group where there is one single figure or cluster of people set up as superior to the rest. Sometimes the control is overt. Sometimes it is subtle. We are all watching a faction try to form now. I truly believe it will not be allowed to form because of the work we do here in the taps I share. I believe we are only showing the process so that we can learn from it. The process uses fear to rally people around a cause to empower those in control even more. Inducing fear is the fastest way to milk people of their energy and attain control.

Those of us who are aware see these dynamics so clearly now. It is useless to try to reason with someone who is immersed in the stupor of psychic streams of energy. It is best to withdraw from engaging them because the self-righteousness and anger that is stoked is the second best way to feed these psychic streams of energy. The types of truth I share dry up these psychic energies. Truth would be available to everyone perhaps if it weren't for the psychic streams of energy keeping people in a stupor.

These energies are very low in quality. They are very easy to dissipate with the understanding of them that I have given. In a way, I am gifting the reader with a reprieve from them. They can peek through the clouds and grasp truth for themselves. They can then awaken from their effects. It is happening more and more. The more people who read my work, the more holes that are poked in these psychic clouds of control. This is how mass awakening is possible. This is how World Peace is formulating.

My posts are a lifeboat to World Peace because these energies are so low on the frequency scale. Love and truth (real love and truth), sear through them like sunshine dries up the morning mist. It is only an illusion that they are powerful. It is a trick of manipulated light shining back in the eyes of the truth seer.

(Say each statement three times while tapping on your head and say it a fourth time while tapping on your chest.)

"I evaporate all psychic streams of energy of rhetoric; in all moments."

"I evaporate all psychic streams of energy of all dictators; in all moments."

"I evaporate all psychic streams of energy of all governments; in all moments."

"I evaporate all psychic streams of energy of all religions; in all moments."

"I evaporate all psychic streams of energy of self-righteousness; in all moments."

"I evaporate all psychic streams of energy of monetary worship; in all moments."

"I evaporate all psychic streams of energy of superiority; in all moments."

"I evaporate all psychic streams of energy of war; in all moments."

"I evaporate all psychic streams of energy that induce hatred; in all moments."

"I evaporate all psychic streams of energy that induce violence; in all moments."

"I evaporate all psychic streams of energy of patriotism; in all moments."

"I evaporate all psychic streams of energy of dysfunction; in all moments."

"I evaporate all psychic streams of energy of caste

systems; in all moments."

"I evaporate all psychic streams of energy of blind faith; in all moments."

"I evaporate all psychic streams of energy of "them versus us" mode; in all moments."

"I evaporate all psychic streams of energy of male domination; in all moments."

"I evaporate all psychic streams of energy of victimhood; in all moments".

"I evaporate all psychic streams of energy of revenge; in all moments."

"I evaporate all psychic streams of energy of poverty; in all moments."

"I evaporate all psychic streams of energy set up by all hierarchies; in all moments."

"I evaporate all psychic streams of unworthiness; in all moments."

"I evaporate all psychic streams of energy of slavery; in all moments."

"I evaporate all psychic streams of energy of servitude; in all moments."

"I evaporate all psychic streams of energy of ignorance; in all moments."

"I evaporate all psychic streams of energy of sexual deviance; in all moments."

"I evaporate all psychic streams of energy of demonizing truth; in all moments."

"I evaporate all psychic streams of energy of reactionary mode; in all moments."

"I evaporate all psychic streams of energy of power; in all moments."

"I evaporate all psychic streams of energy of greed; in all moments."

"I evaporate all psychic streams of energy created by electronics; in all moments."

"I evaporate all psychic streams of energy of mass media; in all moments."

"I evaporate all psychic streams of energy of despair; in all moments."

"I evaporate all psychic streams of energy of hopelessness; in all moments."

"I evaporate all psychic streams of energy of need; in all moments."

"I evaporate all psychic streams of energy of want; in all moments."

"I evaporate all psychic streams of energy of addiction;

in all moments."

"I evaporate all psychic streams of energy of suicide; in all moments."

"I evaporate all psychic streams of energy of big business; in all moments."

"I evaporate all psychic streams of energy of selfishness; in all moments."

"I evaporate all psychic streams of energy of illusion; in all moments."

"I evaporate all psychic streams of energy of primal mode; in all moments."

"I evaporate all psychic streams of energy that hold humanity hostage; in all moments."

Here is a shortlist. It should free people enough so they can start seeing truth more. And since truth and love resonate at similar frequencies, it will allow people to open up and trust love more.

Thank you for your part.

25: EXODUS AND THE LYMPHATIC SYSTEM

There is an emotional issue in the lymphatic system for many people. It is associating being drained to exhaustion with a long exodus that happened in a past life. Think of today's immigrants and what they go through. You have your own experience with that in some form. That is why it is difficult for so many people to have compassion for refugees. It triggers their own past trauma. And with the present one-life whitewash that people use for denial and control, there is no viable way to deal with these issues that come up except denial and dis-ease.

What happens is when you walk or exert your lymphatic system, it triggers the trauma of a drudgery of the long exodus in a past life, maybe to nowhere or to death. The emotional issue of running for your life is held in the endocrine system. A similar thing as with the lymphatic system happens with the endocrine system. When it is ignited, it triggers the past life of running for your life. So it may shut down and work less effectively.

The interesting thing is how the macrocosm (the whole) is triggering the issues held in the microcosm (the individual). The same apathy and indifference that is seen systemically in our ruling parties is the same apathy and indifference we hold in our body that causes our different systems to shut down. Maybe if the world showed more concern for individuals in plight, it would release the memories and issues for individuals' plights.

So maybe this can work in reverse. Maybe if we address our own issues stored in our energy system, it will create a return to ease for many individuals who are suffering in this world. That is why I address the one-life ridiculous notion that was instated during the dark ages and has kept us there.

At this point, I don't care who I offend. I am offended at hearing the cries of humanity go unheeded. I am offended at the systemic display of white pomp and power that is paraded in front of us daily to stroke the ego of the entitled. I am offended by the dumbing down of society merely to perpetuate the profits of a few. I am offended by children being poisoned by mercury and not having their right to pure drinking water mainly because they were born with dark pigment in their skin. I am offended about those in office even uttering reverence for a God when they clearly have little compassion for anyone not in their tax bracket. I am offended.

I am especially offended at going unheard when I speak truth. As soon as I say something that someone doesn't like, they are perched to engage me. It is like dealing with trained monkeys who have been conditioned over the centuries to react on cue and will not recognize a kindness when offered.

Here are some taps that can give you freedom from the issues that go unaddressed within you. I am happy to assist in releasing issues. Perhaps as more people do the taps, others will gain the courage to speak truth instead of going along with the one-life pretense that allows power mongers to go unchecked. Because if they really had to face the fact that they will be returning to the world that they overpopulate, poison and rampage, perhaps they would treat it and others with more care.

(Say each statement three times while tapping on your head and say it a fourth time while tapping on your chest.)

"I release associating activity with the exodus; in all moments."

"I release the trauma and difficulty of the exodus from my lymphatic system; in all moments."

"I release the emotion of "hopeless" from my lymphatic system; in all moments."

"I release the fear of being drained of all my reserve; in

all moments."

"I remove all engrams of the difficulty of the exodus from my beingness; in all moments."

"I release fighting for my life; in all moments."

"I remove all the trauma of fighting for my life from my endocrine system; in all moments."

"I release using up my reserve fighting for my life; in all moments."

"I remove all engrams of fighting for my life from my beingness; in all moments."

26: FREE YOURSELF OF TAKING THAT LAST BREATH

Wouldn't it be great if an individual could share all of their passion with others so that others could rise to the same occasion? It would uplift all of humanity. Isn't that what Martin Luther King, Jr. did with his passionate speeches? Princess Dianna inspired the world with her graciousness and kindness. Rosa Parks seemed to gift humanity with her courage. The world responded and shifted. It is an easy process of sharing. If two phones can share information by being next to each other, why can't two individuals? We actually do it all the time. But people are limited to their linear beliefs, so they negate all the experiences that happen to them in exponential existence.

Even the most sacred experience of love is downgraded in a linear timeline. All the rules that are applied to love make it nearly impossible for someone to receive it if they are adhering to linear rules. So many feel rejected and a failure because of this. By linear rules, you must love one person to fall in love. Falling in love is someone actually experiencing their exponential reality in the linear timeline. You must love family even if they treat you poorly and hate you. It is wrong if you love yourself. The reason that it is set up that you don't love or value yourself is because if you do, you are more apt to understand the spontaneous experience of being ignited into exponential existence.

But it needs to happen. All must relinquish the chains of a limited linear reality if we are going to transcend as a species. We are all watching the chokehold of linear limitations now. Many talk about the limitations all the time. Some are trapped in obsessing over current events. It is like a dying man focusing on taking his next breath. But that is what we are all doing--taking our last breath in linear existence.

It is inevitable that we evolve. We are now like those first sea creatures that finally walked up on land and discovered a greater world of freedom in evolving beyond just the sea. We are evolving beyond the limitations of linear reality. We are stepping into an exponential world where all are ignited in passion and truth is once again relevant.

In exponential existence, love is prevalent, and integrity and truth are mainstays. There is value to all beings and the concept of multiple levels of worthiness is obsolete. Purpose is found in sharing your gifts. The joy of doing something one loves is expounded in sharing. This mainstay replaces being enslaved to money or competition that happens in linear existence.

Everyone is too busy doing what they love and sharing their gifts to have the energy or inclination to judge or diminish others. The sharing of what one loves is the norm. It self-regulates moral conduct. It replaces the need for a monetary system.

People who are reading this can gauge how trapped they are in linear existence or how free they are in exponential reality by how they respond to it. Those who accept it easily are perhaps already experiencing such freedom. Those who have trouble with this are still immersed in a linear reality and cannot see the upgrade in consciousness.

All is well. We will all get there. But just as one individual can change the course of the world, I use my intention to expound everyone into exponential existence. I am the phone that is held out to share its data with the next phone. Yet I share it with all inhabitants. This is what female empowerment affords me. What would never occur to male energy to do, female energy does easily. Male energy holds onto the boundaries of the self as tightly as an insecure tyrant. Female energy expands her intention to nurture all life.

Perhaps having male energy so concentrated right now affords female energy the ability to dominate the expansiveness of the opposite pole of giving right now. Perhaps the reason for male energy doing what it is doing right now is so that I can do what I do I in female empowerment. As male energy is abusing itself with humanity at its mercy, perhaps female energy is free to expound all her awareness onto the masses to create the evolutionary shift necessary. Female energy is free to nurture all and abide by her natural inclinations.

So here I am expanding my energy to gift anyone who is willing to partake. I expand my consciousness (love) to permeate the whole planet and to gift anyone who is receptive to the sanctity of truth and love. May one feel inspired, healed, rejuvenated, awakened, benevolent, worthy and gracious to all life. May all be grateful for the experience of existing. May anyone and everyone, as they are inspired, stretch themselves across the world. May we all offer new hope and freedom to the land and free all of judgment and control.

27: THE HEART CHAKRA OF THE UNIVERSE

The fluidity of humanity is in its creativity. It is also in its joy, love, abundance and freedom. Those with an agenda have us fixate on problems of the world to prevent us from enjoying the fluidity of life. Humanity is all coagulated. The stringent moral beliefs of different sects dry up the sap of its creativity. We are all aware enough now to be a witness to that.

Many people question what they have been told about the hereafter. But they also are forbidden by their doctrine to believe in alternative worlds or reincarnation. They are paralyzed in an indifference of denial. If you can honestly talk to someone about what they truly believe, they will tell you they don't believe in the traditional heaven. But when you press them further, they will shrug and get defensive. They are terrified to go against the conditioning of their sect.

This is the behavior of someone who is trapped between a rock and a hard place. That is what society has done to all its inhabitants. It is not free to express its inner promptings of what its innate intelligence is telling it. It is not free to delve into all the experiences it carries the memory of within, like a treasure trove.

Universal peace can't happen unless a majority of individuals attain inner peace, for we are all a mini schematic (microcosm) of the whole (macrocosm). Having everyone fixated on outer problems and turmoil is actually a calculated intention of keeping people enslaved to the turmoil. All of humanity is like a self-holding trap. The more we struggle, the more we hold ourselves trapped. The escape is to totally relax and allow your energy to drop out.

What is interesting about humans is they share more information than they realize. We are all symbiotic that way. An energy field is not dead energy. It is emitting frequencies and information faster than the human brain can receive. That is all being psychic really is-- being able to read the energy signals that an energy field is putting out without having to wait for it to be translated into language. This is slow and clumsy. We are all outgrowing the need for such cumbersome communications.

If you want to facilitate the advancement to Universal peace, gain peace within yourself. Honor peace as if the sanctity of all of life depends upon it because it does. What you choose for your thoughts, feelings, speech and actions is averaged into the collective. The more individuals that can choose positive and productive thoughts, feelings, speech and actions, the more all of humanity will respond.

Better yet, if one can practice the neutrality of Divine Love without putting a judgment or spin on it, the more quickly this world will flourish into a blossoming universal expression of Truth and Love.

I was explaining this process to one very advanced soul. He was indifferent. I could see his thought energy. He was reading indifference. He did not care. He could travel to any of a few wonderful planets that were better suited to him than earth. He had little investment in earth and resented being here. Here was this spiritually advanced individual, and he was as indifferent as people immersed in the indifference of thinking they only live one life.

I immediately tuned into the Ancient Ones and asked them how to make him understand that earth mattered. They revealed a new truth to me. Earth is very important to the wellbeing of all the planets he visited. There was a reason so many advanced individuals had incarnated on this planet. It is the heart chakra of the Universe. To open all the lower worlds to love, the earth needed to be opened up unquestionably to love.

Many spiritual beings were led into indifference by the belief that this is a warring planet and there is no point in trying to uplift the consciousness. This was an intentional attempt to enslave all in the lower worlds to indifference. They were taught to focus on themselves because spirituality is an individual experience. They were given half-truths to enslave them in indifference. It has been a means of putting a glass ceiling on the most advanced spiritual beings and trapping them in the mental realms.

I see many people whom I respected years ago as dynamic energy now milling around in the mental realms. They scan social media for anyone who believes differently than they do and engage them in a hearty debate. They are intending to lure people to their belief, which they have been taught, is the way to truth. But as anyone can tell spiritually, it merely leads to a cul de sac in the mental realms.

These dynamic individuals are seen as ineffective as spiritual mavericks. And they do not see it within themselves, but if they are capable of being honest with themselves, they see it in other members of their belief system. In a way, it is more tragic than pure ignorance because there is little way to reach these individuals unless love and truth are able to bore through the mental trap. So the Ancient Ones feed truth into someone like myself whom no one listens to, no one respects and no one values. Someone who clearly is removed from all that brings anyone esteem in this world. They hide truth in plain sight. Then they observe who is able to get past their own objections to find it.

This guise is brilliant: to be able to write all the truths that have sieved out of humanity without anyone being the wiser except those who can get past their own ego. When someone first comes to my page, they may have such contempt for me that it is painful to tolerate. But once one truth gets through, it shifts them a little and then they are easier to engage. This happens continually.

There is a reason that I am in a female body. It is true that it is much easier to catch the attention of others in a male body. And anyone in a male body will tell you that a male body is necessary to assist others to their empowerment. It has better defenses against the blows and onslaught of contempt. But male energy is not the only embodiment to serve in. This we now know is a lie because many have been led to their empowerment through my assistance.

It is much more difficult in a female body though. It is excruciating. It takes a strength and endurance that a male body cannot fathom. The sensitivities to what a female body can endure are much more extreme than a male body could even withstand. A male body would wave it off and be done with it. That is its grace. A female energy must expand herself even further to endure the coarse thoughts, feelings and actions of all that are within her realm. She does not dismiss anyone. All are worthy. No one is a throw away.

It is not her nature to turn anyone away or to dismiss them. It is not her nature to influence where they go energetically. She does not collect followers to sit at her feet. She gives all of herself to all that she loves and blesses them in every direction with her loving protection wherever they go. She does not collect followers at all like marbles in a jar. She expands her consciousness as far as necessary to love everyone where they are.

That year when I was imprisoned, starved and tortured, I went through enlightenment. I was fascinated by the depths of my connection to something I was not able to formulate because of the conditioning of the torture. But I knew I was connected and protected somehow. I remember burning my arm on the side of the iron furnace every night. I watched as my arm formulated a welt or blister from the furnace, and I didn't feel a thing. I felt no pain.

That is the level of pain and diligence it takes to pour truth and love into the world. I didn't realize at the time what an analogy that was for my future. I tend the world day and night fueling it with love and truth so that the last embers of such do not die out in the world. I try to ignite flames of empowerment with my writings and posts continuously watching them catch flame and then dampen with indifference, all the while protected and numbed of the excruciating pain associated with the process.

Want to hear the most ridiculous part? No one takes me seriously. Not even anyone I have assisted, healed or proved myself to unless I preference truth with saying that I am speaking to my Guides which, of course, people construe as a panel of men. Think about it. That is how deep the conditioning away from the empowerment of a balance between male and female energy goes.

Even a dynamic healer needs to defer to a panel of men to be deemed legitimate. This is how deep the conditioning goes. This is why it is so important to live, see, breathe and sleep truth, but most of all to speak it so that others may know truth without having to suffer for the privilege.

I love you all. You are worth EVERYTHING.

28: YOUR VALIDATION

The human consciousness is so dense. I have been wasting so much energy merely wanting to fit in. I have been wondering why some people have this aversion to me. All I ever wanted was to have a big family. Being rejected by my own family one by one and being seen as the instigator, growing up with no friends, not attracting relationships, and causing nice people to have hostility toward me and target me has been the norm.

Since I went through enlightenment and was starved and tortured for a year, I have been living in solitude. I thought that would somehow change. But I had an epiphany at the dog park today.

I thought I could just go to the dog park and enjoy taking my dogs and blend. But that is not the case. When I go to the park, the whole place is emptied. People don't want their dogs playing with mine, and people seem to avoid me at all costs. I am not being paranoid. This is really happening. It is really unkind of me to show up there at this point.

I am told by my Guides that I do not have the luxury of being part of the herd anymore. I came here specifically as a conduit for truth and a wayshower of love. I have been wasting all this energy trying to figure out why people don't like me. It is simply that this world has an aversion to truth. It takes all my stamina and talents to just simply keep sharing truths. The frequency of truth that I resonate with actually irritates most people. Perhaps truth in them is stirred up and they react to the lack of truth that we have been immersed in.

So I will stop wasting energy trying to fit in, and it will free up more energy to pour truth into the world. Love and truth resonate similarly. So the more truth this world can withstand, the more love it can withstand as well.

I will accept my role more willingly as a wayshower and stop denying that I am being used in this way. It is the only thing that makes sense in this world. The love that I intend for you may seem like a luxury to those who feel similarly to me. It is because we are meant to take our individual empowerment back. This can't happen when it is averaged in a group. So if you are feeling lonely, rejected, isolated, misunderstood and unsupported, all are true, but only in the old dynamics.

In a greater way, you are loved, supported and encouraged to be the exponential dynamo that you are. Instead of feeling rejected, reject all notions that others need to approve of you for you to get validation. In fact, the opposite is true. If you are feeling invalidated, it is proof in itself that you are closer to the heartbeat of love. For look at what is popular right now and be grateful you are not of that limited caliber. Let that be your validation.

29: HOW WE AWAKEN

Healing is a perpetual task with some people. It is very easy for me to take away the stagnant energy of an issue. It is simply a matter of pulling it out with a pure intention. The difficult part is in preventing the person from reclaiming it as soon as it is removed.

They want to talk about how awful the situation is and how much it burdened them. In doing that, they are pulling it back. It is no different than collecting items from a hoarder to remove and having them snatch the items back out of the pile.

Removing someone's issue can make them resent you like the hoarder resents you helping them get rid of the extra load. As much as I explain to them afterwards not to pull back the issues by talking about them, many cannot help themselves. When I am adamant, they believe I am rude for not allowing them to speak. I am fighting for their freedom harder than they are capable of realizing it.

This is why I can't talk to a client after they have just

had a session with me. Even the most aware people will slip their hand in the pile and try to pull back the issue. Preventing them from doing so many times requires more effort than the actual releasing of the issue.

If people could take heart to understand this one thing, most people could release their own issues. It is a matter of identifying too closely with this concept of self, the ego. The purpose of heart-wrenching pain is to pull yourself from identifying too strongly with the vantage point of you.

Try to think of your physical self as merely your vehicle to hold space in the physical world. Everything you hold onto as a concept of yourself has to be carried around in the "backseat." When someone hurts your feelings or a situation causes you to feel pain, think of it as a way of showing you how cluttered your car is. People who believe that they are mostly a physical body will stuff every belief and interpersonal dynamic in their little vehicle. It weighs them down. There is a different way to approach life.

The absolutes that we are innately taught in society condition us to a limited experience of living. I hear people say that family is everything. The people who have been family members in this life to me have worked overtime to diminish and discredit me at every turn. It is because we have been enemies in a past life and they have been "packed" around me to create such resistance in me that I have become incredibly strong in moving through that resistance. It has strengthened me to be able to share such incredible truth here with less wear and tear on me.

If I were to subscribe to that one belief--that family is everything--my purpose would have been halted right there. Another belief is that you have to be in a male body to dispense truth at the highest level. Of course, that goes unchallenged by so many and they put a glass ceiling on themselves. Female energy is endowed with all the love and compassion that is the embodiment of higher truth. Why would a woman NOT be able to sustain such presence in the physical realm? Female energy attributes are more akin to the subtle realms. This is a glass ceiling that people have put on their teachings.

If a physical person on a spiritual quest was like a rocket being thrust into space, the male energy would be like the nose of the rocket that propels them through the coarse layers of space and then breaks off and is discarded. Female energy would be more suited to float suspended in the higher realms. Both are necessary. Female energy without its male counterpart may be ineffective in the coarse vibration of this world. Male energy disconnected from its female counterpart can be the brute. This is what we have been systemically seeing played out in the world in both men and women.

When everyone is screaming at each other in protest, voicing their opinion, beating down the opposition, it can be disheartening. But in a way, it is exciting to see many of those in female energy reclaiming their voice by protesting. In that way, it is a positive thing. They are coming in balance with their male energy. Sure, it is messy and uncomfortable. Much of growth can be awkward and confusing.

For those who have been predominately male energy, a way for them to come to terms with their female energy counterpart is through self-reflection. Male energy does not think about much outside of results. If people were to challenge themselves, they would reflect on other experiences outside of the realm of their present possibility and get a sense of what those in other "cars" were experiencing.

All the browbeating, manipulating and control that is now being demonstrated in the world is a way to blow off the final reserve of male energy domination that has been running the planet to the ground. Let the people blow their wad of collected "power." Power is no longer a monetary system of the new earth.

We are all getting a ringside view of its disgusting displays of strutting and bragging. Enjoy the show. In fact, many of us have been waiting lifetime upon lifetime to have such aggressive displays of power be seen for what they really are. Beyond the billows of male energy being displayed is the soothing sense of wonderment for all to explore.

Do you notice how the old ways of entertaining yourself in the facade of this world are no longer as satisfying? Everything in the media is being seen for what it has been all along. It has been a subtle programming to lead us all to war, violence and self-sabotage. Even if you go to a toy store, you will see many toys are a means to play violently.

This is no coincidence. This is what we have been conditioned to believe is natural. The subtleties of this tactic have been lost because of male energy's desperation to remain dominant. In fact, just in writing this and having some realize this truth, more of the facade is ripped off. The power of male dominance is like a scab loosely clinging on the skinned knee of humanity. It is inevitable that it be ripped off; everyone is waiting to witness the fresh new skin of a new earth underneath.

Look at the age-old practice of pumping our children with toxic sugar as a means to celebrate every sacred event. Society has been programmed that this is normal. Try not practicing such rituals with those who are used to it. But even this is coming to an end. We have stretched the envelope to how many toxins we can add to foods. Soon people will be clamoring for the nutrients they now may miss out on and realize the emptiness of empty consumption.

People are awakening to the facade of this manufactured reality. Before it is too late, they are going to recognize the benevolence of nature and the wisdom of trees and advocate for it just as strongly and vehemently as now happens with the killing sticks that male energy so dearly reveres.

It happens because we are now awakening to the fact that we are not only what is in our "car." We move around and have the ability to interact in such sacred subtle levels that it is difficult to deny. That is what I do with all of you. If you are lonely or despondent, I can come to you in energy and comfort you not because I am superhuman but because I understand our true nature. You are awakening to this nature too.

I understand how you have been duped, betrayed, demoralized, humiliated, and worn down to a nub. I know how you have been swayed and convinced that you are broken. I know how you have been conditioned to lose hope. But I also know the resilience of the human spirit. It lies in the awakening of your female empowerment. You are stronger than a mountain, fluid as an ocean and as resilient as a willow. You are good, whole, pure, aware, realized and blessed. You come by this honestly from within. It is not something you have to be deemed worthy of by any male influence. It is your true nature.

Certainly, male energy without its counterpart is broken. It needed to be. But we, of the gaining numbers of the awakening, are here to pour enthusiasm and healing into the cracks of an overtaxed culture. Female energy is the balm and the cure for all that ails a dying race.

By claiming our compassion and intuition and gaining insight through our imagination, we reclaim our empowerment and, in doing so, we reclaim humanity. Transcendence will never happen through male energy alone (might versus right). It will be done by conceding to the sweetness and cadence of life itself. By honoring the greatness of the cricket while he still strokes his instrument. Honoring the trees as they reach out to imbue us with their insights. It is done by embracing that benevolence within ourselves by seeing it reflected in all others.

We are the great souls that came here to save humanity. We do so simply by sharing our special gifts of kindness, compassion, and healing as best as we can. In doing so, we fulfill our purpose. In doing so, we heal our ailing planet. In doing so, we manifest World Peace.

30: IF YOU VALUE TREES, OR HOW TO BE A WORLD SAVIOR

If you value trees, you better stop being ashamed that you connect with them, that they comfort you, that you sense their wisdom and that they are sentient beings. The lens of the human consciousness is so rigid and dense that unless you help people turn their lens by sharing what you are aware of, theirs will stay in a closed position.

TREES OF THE WORD BESEECH YOU

Sure technology could synthesize air. That is what many companies may wish. So if you are shy about what you know about trees and how they have assisted you to thrive, that experience could be lost to us all. It may have been hard to imagine a few short months ago, but now your resistance to sharing your awareness may be detrimental in saving our planet.

Humans are very selfish beings when their lens is closed. You have to make them want what you have. That is the key. Be vocal about the intangible relationship you have with trees so much so that it will catch on to those not yet awakened. Trees matter. Trees have a dynamic presence, wisdom and individuality in each. Trees have kindness and compassion that many humans seem incapable of. The beautiful poetry I write is actually the transcription of certain trees. Some are more poetic than others.

I don't care who thinks this is silly. I care about those who will find courage to speak about their dynamics with trees before trees are exploited to extinction. It really is up to you in getting over your fear of seeming strange. This fear was a calculated tactic to keep people enslaved. Why is it such a bad thing to be a tree hugger?

I created the social media page "Wisdom of the Trees" as an interface between trees and man. It never caught on because the humans could not fathom it. I started it when I started a forest in my kitchen, and the trees and the saplings told me many things because of my efforts. They were excited when humans got social media because humans could finally understand how trees communicate. It is similar to the Internet but through their root systems.

But as humans upgrade in their abilities, they entrench in their ignorance. They are afraid of evolving beyond their comfort zone so they hold on to old ideas and ideologies. One of them is that trees are lifeless beings. Another is that it is dangerous to acknowledge trees.

One more that seems irrelevant to this topic but is not, is reincarnation.

Humans carry in their DNA memories of their past lives. It is imprinted on the fetus what they will become and creates the background story of each baby that is born. That is why babies are so different. Some are born sickly, some are gifted. Many are in the average range. The experience that a person has is influenced by the imprint of past lives on their DNA. It is why some children are so devastatingly different from their parents, or why an adopted baby gets exactly the right parents. The past lives create the framework for this life.

People think that DNA is set in stone. But this is not true. It is a fluid system as well. Imprints can be dented out. Some people can evolve more quickly or break out of their framed experiences the more they think for themselves, are positive and go off autopilot. This actually changes their genetic propensity. Genetic diseases are the opposite of positive. They are merely emotional issues that get stored in the DNA and are then passed down to the baby.

These issues can be released in hindsight and the genetic diseases can clear up. Technology probably already has an understanding of this. But along with fossil fuel and a belief in just one lifetime, we are shackled to these issues for someone to make a profit and to control the masses. So sustainable energy, alternative healing practices and the concept of reincarnation are all demonized for the benefit of control. It is up to the individuals to challenge such things, so a tipping point can happen in the course of humanity and we can transcend the ridiculousness. Even Jesus talked about reincarnation way back then.

The primal fear in standing up for trees comes from an era when the Druids and pagans communicated with trees and had a deep interconnection with them. These peaceful people were lumped into one group with barbarians who plundered the land. It was an easy genocide for those who were killing in the name of God to get rid of pagans.

This is where so much hesitancy comes in about not challenging someone's religious beliefs. It is not always respect but fear. One may fear speaking their truth if they hold the memory of being tortured and killed as a heretic for not following Jesus Christ or for loving trees. Also, those who were on the side of the genocide may have an aversion to alternative practices because they trigger in them that primal hate of pagans.

When someone calls someone a tree hugger, they are poking a stick at this past life wound of being a peaceful tree lover. They were really so easy to kill off. It made ruthless men feel empowered at its ease. That ruthless power comes to the surface still when they mock someone for being a tree hugger. They are basically saying, "We killed you in the past for talking to trees. We will do it again."

So these fears of talking to trees is earned honestly. So is the ruthless mocking of what one does not understand. Both sides have painful pasts to tend with (if we ever do acknowledge such things). Perhaps the drive to stay in denial about one's own actions makes it easier not to acknowledge reincarnation. Everyone wants to be the innocent. With the concept of one life securely in place, no one ever has to be held accountable for how their past transgressions led to the current state of the world.

But for those of us who believe that the world is worth saving, we will do whatever we can do to awaken the masses. Maybe by stepping out of our comfort zone and admitting our special relationship with trees, we will be healing an old wound and overcoming an ancient fear. Perhaps by simply being present in our own understanding of truth, we will help sway public understanding of trees, natural healing and reincarnation. Perhaps in this way, we can all consider ourselves world saviors.

People wonder how I tap into truth. The trees tell me. Trees love you.

31: REMOVING SHACKLES UPON TRUTH

There are some things that very spiritual people believe without question that are glass ceilings on truth. They are, in fact, hindering the progression of all humanity. If the most spiritual people on the planet are accepting half truths as whole truths, then they are bottlenecking all of humanity into a limited state of consciousness. I sit back and say nothing out of respect for people's beliefs, but if someone is enslaved, do you give deference to the prison?

If people have come into this lifetime to seek truth, then seek it. Any outside source, including myself, that tells you something which causes tightness in your stomach or your chest, must be challenged. It means that there is an inconsistency between your external compass and absolute truth. Absolute truth does change. It needs to stay at least as fluid as water so as not to be stagnant. Some really shining souls are wading through stagnant pools out of loyalty.

One must challenge who and what they are being loyal to. Truth never expects blind loyalty. Truth never stops at a fixed view. There are absolutely no absolutes with truth. It keeps weaving and flowing, breaking down the facade that is its own deposit. Lime builds up as a natural deposit of flowing water moving over rock. Facades build up as a natural process of truth washing over the likes of men. Good people get caught up in the formations. That is when truth is forced to break out in a new way and wash away what once held it up because that barrier has proved to then hold truth back. Truth will not allow it.

I am not a brave soul. I have been diminished and attacked on all sides in all ways. Life and people have washed me clean of all want, hope and need. The only compulsion is to share truth and to heal the injustices served to so many.

So many think that truth is the same as an opinion. So they attack me with contempt because in their humble opinion I am wrong. By the way, there is nothing humble about an opinion. It is arrogance realizing it is arrogant and so wears the cloak of humility to slip past anyone who is as clever as it is.

I share things that I know. Having forgone any sense of being socially embraced, I have sat and watched humanity on the sidelines. I have gleaned love and comfort from wise intangible advisers who loved me and made me feel safe when no human could bother to do so. It is these ancient beings to whom I speak regularly and who have gotten me to this point of even having a voice.

I speak to others out there who are ruthlessly devoted to a higher purpose, who aren't adorned simply for showing up, who are not welcome into groups and situations with open arms, have been given disdain simply for existing and have not had the good fortune of being born into a place of stature.

Some of us have complied with a notch in the world simply because they have accepted us in. Some have been coaxed into a group that seemed to provide the answers to all our questions. But no group really does that. No group puts the individual above the purpose of the group except at first to coax them in. But then there is a complacency that is replaced with truth seeking. That complacency is the shackles upon truth.

So here are some beliefs that I would like to challenge. The Ancient Ones have been working with me a long time to give me the courage to do this. But truth must be won and re-won. Truth is not found in any hierarchy, group or galvanized belief system.

Here are things that I would challenge any seeker of truth to look at:

- If you can see things in the beliefs of someone else that seem ridiculous, it means that there are things in your own belief system that are ridiculous as well. If receiving seventy two virgins in heaven for martyring yourself seems far-fetched, look at what is in your own faith that was put there to manipulate you as well.

- Any belief that was established in a male dominated world is based on a lie because all of humanity has been skewed to a lie. The belief that a woman cannot be the leader of a religion because of the molecular make up of her atoms is a lie. At that level of awareness, a person can change their molecular make up. I release genetic issues from people all the time, so it must be possible for a female to be everything a male is in energy and more.

- People don't need to struggle on their own to learn their spiritual lessons. That is a lie given to spiritually savvy people so they won't end the suffering that power feeds on. We have all been around the block spiritually. If we haven't learned our lessons, it means that we are trapped in some way. It is only the humane thing to do to release someone from their cage. It is a callous indifference not to help someone you are able to help. I was taught that it was wrong in a spiritual group to use my skills to heal others. It was only through much coaxing by my ancient advisers that I overcame this apprehension.

- The Universe is not a warring Universe, and this does not have to be a warring planet. That view was inflicted on the world by a very sincere spiritual seeker who regrets that he has created complacency in the world by his limited view at the time. He had a very difficult existence here on earth as I have. I understand the conflicts that he endured to love so deeply and to be invalidated so greatly. I understand. He and I are kindred spirits. He regrets that this view was inflicted on the world through the human eyes of contempt. If you can expand your vision further, you can see the peace and tranquility of space that is hinted of in nature. If you have a connection with this soul, he will affirm this truth.

- I get attacked a lot by people of a spiritual group for speaking truth. What I say resonates as truth to them, but they are so fearful of going against their leader that they curse the mouth of truth. They blindly give homage to someone who should be feeding them truth on a regular basis. I have been put in the position of sharing truths that are not coming from the mouths of religious leaders. People hardly know what integrity, honesty, truth and kindness look like anymore. Some have taken willingly of my generosity and insulted me greatly by giving the credit of all I do to their leader. Truth is not a doormat. I cannot politely concede anymore because people are being deprived of truth in the process. That cannot happen.

- When you compare anyone to anyone you have insulted at least one of them. Individuality is where we all shine and when you compare them to someone else or strap someone else on top of them, you have just diminished them greatly. Two rays of sun are equal but they don't emanate in the same direction. Comparing two things is expecting them to emanate in the same way. Who is more connected to wisdom: Mozart or Lady Gaga? There is no comparison. Doing so insults their individuality and stunts their range.

- You don't have to be afraid of taking on karma. Fear is the thing that makes people susceptible. If there is fear there, don't do anything until the love supersedes the fear. The law of love transcends all other experiences so as long as there is love, there is a natural protection.

- All groups are energetic Ponzi schemes. All groups. A Ponzi scheme takes all your assets and distributes them just enough for you to comply. This is being done energetically. Also, there are groups that say they take away all your sins or karma for you so that when you cross over you are free never to have to come back. This is a lie. They instill fear in you that if you leave the group, you will be bombarded with all your karma. This is a scare tactic. It is a curse. It is as much of a lie as the belief you are going to hell if you don't comply.

What does happen in these groups is that new people's karma is taken and distributed amongst everyone. When someone has a hard time, they are said to be burning off karma. They are. They are being given the karma of others to burn off. It is no different than being made to wash the dirty laundry of everyone else in the group. This is a grave injustice to individuality.

There is a way to pass off all karma through a passageway through the human energy makeup where the microcosm converts into the macrocosm. But it doesn't seem to be happening in any groups on earth. It is a very individual process that individuals can learn to do for themselves. But to have someone else take on responsibility for others is a lie. It can be taught and will become second nature, but the cap has to be ripped off truth for that to happen.

There is so much more to say. People bring their engrams of their old religions into new groups and eventually wear them out like old shoes. When I see anyone putting me on a pedestal, I have to remind them that I am flawed and inadequate to adorn. Everyone is. That adornment ruins the most noble of causes. It creates superficiality and breeds superiority. Spirituality is not a multilevel marketing scheme. People share their gifts in such non-linear ways that to compartmentalize them in any way does humanity a disservice.

If any group tells you that you are special for being in it, run away. This is stroking the ego. There are spiritual groups out there who tell people that they are the chosen ones. One of the purposes of these groups is to attract psychically savvy individuals and keep them trapped in compliance from harming others with their abilities. It works but is less necessary than it once was. The Universe strengthens as all individuals accept their omnipotence.

Any group that keeps secrets is outmoded. I share truth without making people pay a fee or give allegiance or subscribe to a doctrine. I do this so the playing field can be leveled and all can have access to truth. I am amazed at how many people scoff or reject this gift, but I understand the extreme conditioning that they have endured to get to this point.

There is so much more to say but it is irrelevant if no one wants to hear it. For those who are, or once considered themselves truth seekers, I hope these words resonate as an opening of a cage door. In past eras, they would have been used as dangling carrots to intrigue souls, but they are stated now to free souls.

That is my only intention in writing them, or should I say, the only intention of the Ancient Ones in having me write this. They work diligently on opening all souls up to truth. They resent when any group tries to own them as mascots for the unworthy agenda of putting a cap on truth. Ask them yourself. They will tell you the same thing.

They love you. I love you. Existence is love itself.

32: HOW DO I TELL?

Someone asked how I determine which one of my books is right for them. I am a medical intuitive, which means I can tune into the body and see where there is something off physically. But I am an intuitive of more subtle aspects of a person as well.

I can tune into their emotions, Akashic records, and mental make-up to see what is off in these areas as well. Each aspect of a person is a different layer of "frequency" or vibration. When there are holes in their auras (layers of energy), schisms, or unaligned aspects, I can see it. Some who have been devastated have broken aspects of them. I can see scars from past lives, and I can see when someone's energy field is simply shattered or blown away.

What I am constantly doing with my love, voice, presence and intention is repairing energy fields of people, animals, places, situations, the earth and all of existence with a perpetual love, which is an energy that I have trained myself to emanate from me, like a fountain into all of life.

So when I see someone's name, I can tap into their vibration and see what they are open to. It is like looking at a person and being able to see what kind of music they are most apt to listen to based on their appearance. I see their pain, resistance, thought process, desperate need to repair their relationship with energy and their own capabilities that they have been sitting on because it has not been acceptable in society to share.

My books are not merely words to read. They are a healing vibration. When someone decides to read one of my books, they are taking the initiative to empower themselves. It doesn't matter if it is the poetry book (*Children of The Universe*), quote book (*Grow Where You Are Planted*), the book on subtle truths society has withheld (*Letters of Accord*), the food issue book (*Do What You Love Diet*) or the tapping books (*Enlightenment Unveiled, Perpetual Calendar* and *Emerging From the Mist*).

Reading any of my books is like taking an initiation in some secret sect. Because in a male based society, truth was shared only with those who were deemed worthy. Who decided you were worthy? Men. In the awakening of the consciousness, female attributes must flood the world and regain a place in society to balance out the ruthlessness of man. These things are kindness, compassion, support, understanding, integrity, and honesty.

In a female society, who decides you are worthy? You.

In a female/male balanced society, there is no longer a need for false humility because people are no longer pitted against each other in a perpetual competition.

Everyone exists in an aspect of sisterhood. It is an existence where everyone is rooting for each other to succeed. Some people may have experienced this in very closed or small groups. That is why it seems so unfathomable. The concepts of morality and kindness have been arbitrarily weeded out of existence by those who wish to control societal dynamics or even the fate of the world.

These intentions could have started out innocently enough to keep all those in a group safely rounded up with similar beliefs and distinctions. This may have kept them safe from enemies. But at some point it became profitable for someone, in some way, to have enemies, and the system of using beliefs to keep the tribe pure were used to make distinctions between those of the tribe and outsiders. We see these tactics desperately being used by those in power to prevent the world from balancing itself out. That is why the truths I share so desperately are needed for one to awaken to their own empowerment.

We have been privy to a global society that is lacking positive moral traits. When I talk about female empowerment, I am talking about these traits. Nobody with awareness is ever talking about genitals. That is just the coarse understanding of male and female energy that most of us have evolved beyond.

Now it is a matter of realizing it. Everyone needs to awaken to the morality that female empowerment mandates, if not specifically within themselves, at least in their circle of influence and beyond.

So if anyone wants to know which book of mine will assist their awakening the best, I am happy to jump start the process by telling them. Now, more than ever, the world needs every heart to absorb truth and emanate it to the collective of humanity. Thank you for doing that.

33: FORGO THE WIELDING OF POWER

It is such an enlightening commonality that so many are feeling dread at the current events. We believe it is because of politics. This is not necessarily true. What we are experiencing is the dread in realizing that any one person is not worthy to hold such power over the lives of others. The human consciousness is too fickle. We merely have great examples right now as a spiritual teaching prop of how dangerous it is for power to be wielded at all.

The Universe is prompting us to return to love. It is prompting us to return to balance. The Universe is actually giving us an ultimatum that states: If you want to survive on this planet, you better figure it out quick. Will any others heed the call?

Female energy does not solve the issue by marching as male energy would. This is simply female energy doing male energy without the genitals. The saving of the planet is in understanding what divine goddess energy is and emulating it. Its strength is not in pure might, but in resilience, compassion, kindness, cunning and expansion in understanding. There are so few examples of female empowerment that it is difficult to figure out.

Perhaps continue to do the taps and think to yourself what would Grandma Willow from Pocahontas do? Having a fictional character that is not even depicted as human is the only way that male energy has allowed female empowerment to be depicted.

If you have been anxious at the upcoming inauguration and the ramifications of it, these should ease your angst. Writing them and sharing them eased mine.

If you know of anyone who is anxious for the upcoming events, these taps can do more than ease their mind. These taps can bring back a balance to something that has become an abomination to individuality.

(Say each statement three times while tapping on your head and say it a fourth time while tapping on your chest.)

"I declare myself a surrogate for humanity in doing these taps; in all moments."

"I release endorsing the wielding of power; in all moments."

"I release accepting the wielding of power; in all moments."

"I release being a pawn for the wielding of power; in all

moments."

"I release the belief that I am insignificant in the wielding of power; in all moments."

"I nullify all contracts with the wielding of power; in all moments."

"I withdraw all my energy from the wielding of power; in all moments."

"I extract all the support and enthusiasm that I have invested into the wielding of power; in all moments."

"I dry up all psychic streams that mandate the wielding of power; in all moments."

"I send all energy matrices into the Light and Sound that mandate the wielding of power; in all moments."

"I command all complex energy matrices that mandate the wielding of power to be escorted into the Light and Sound by my Guides; in all moments."

"I remove all engrams of the wielding of power; in all moments."

"I remove all programming and conditioning that the wielding of power has put on me; in all moments."

"I strip all illusion off of the wielding of power; in all moments."

"I remove all masks, walls and armor off the wielding

of power; in all moments."

"I eliminate the first cause in regard to the wielding of power; in all moments."

"I release being a party to the wielding of power; in all moments."

"I untangle all my energy from the wielding of power; in all moments."

"I release the genetic propensity to propagate the wielding of power; in all moments."

"I dissolve all of the wielding of power with the purity of Divine Love; in all moments."

"I remove all vortexes between myself and the wielding of power; in all moments."

"I dry up all instincts to participate in the wielding of power; in all moments."

"I recant all vows and agreements between myself and the wielding of power; in all moments."

"I remove all curses between myself and the wielding of power; in all moments."

"I remove all blessings between myself and the wielding of power; in all moments."

"I sever all strings and cords between myself and the wielding of power; in all moments."

"I dissolve all karmic ties between myself and the wielding of power; in all moments."

"I remove all the pain, burden, and limitations that the wielding of power has put on me; in all moments."

"I remove all the fear, futility, and unworthiness that the wielding of power has put on me; in all moments."

"I remove the illusion of isolation or separation that the wielding of power has put on me; in all moments."

"I give back all that I have taken from all others due to the wielding of power; in all moments."

"I extract all of the wielding of power from my Sound frequency and the Universal Sound frequency; in all moments."

"I extract all of the wielding of power from my Light emanation and the Universal Light Emanation; in all moments."

"I release resonating or emanating with the wielding of power; in all moments."

"I transcend the wielding of power; in all moments."

"I collapse and dissolve the wielding of power; in all moments."

"I shift my paradigm from the wielding of power to the empowerment of all individuals in Universal peace; in

all moments."

"I am centered and empowered in the empowerment of all individuals in Universal peace; in all moments."

"I resonate, emanate and am interconnected with all life in the empowerment of all individuals in Universal peace; in all moments."

Let love prevail by simply getting everything out of its way.

34: THE SAVING GRACE OF HUMANITY

I watched my sweet little boy catch a mouse outside the patio window. I have saved mice from him when he was younger. He didn't want to kill it. He just wanted to play and then he wanted to get it out of the house. He is no killer. That is what I told myself. But here he was with a mouse in his mouth tossing it around. I sat there and watched how to interrupt the process and save the mouse. He was already gone. There was no one to save. Just the little carcass that my kitty was so proud of.

I thought about this dilemma. How do I allow my cat to play outside if he is going to kill? I don't believe in taking life. So if I even let him go outside, am I not being compliant? Also, how can I not now judge my sweet baby as a killer? A voice of reason within myself interjected.

The cat killed because he was triggered into the primal mode of killing by circumstance. When he is outside with all the field mice around, he is going to chase and kill them. That is his nature. But when he comes inside, he is my sweet baby again. That is his true nature.

I thought about this in regards to people. Maybe they

are the same way. Maybe they only are ruthless killers when they are triggered into primal mode. Maybe some outside intelligence that controls the dynamics of society knows this too. Maybe that is why they push for every household to have guns. Maybe this is their way to keep us in primal mode and forgo our true nature. Maybe this is how or why they induce us to treating others with total disrespect and contention.

Maybe the inflow of guns, drugs, explicit sex imagery is all a means with one particular motive: to keep humans trapped in primal mode. Primal mode is a knee jerk reactionary state. It doesn't afford those trapped in it the luxury of caring about those that they accost. Perhaps those who control society benefit financially from people staying in primal mode. So they allow the flooding of triggers into society to advance their agenda.

If so, then it is up to individuals to catch on to this and bow out of the situation that they are put in. My sweet cat Willy can't come in from the patio to take himself out of primal mode. He may not even want to. It is fun to catch mice. It is exciting and gets all the adrenaline pumping. It is enjoyable to him when he is out there, to kill mice. He may never want to stop. He can't interrupt the process for himself. But we, as humans, can. The only time he wants to come in, is when he is tired and wants to rest.

Those of us who have long memories of our experiences are tired and want to rest too. We have pulled ourselves out of primal mode simply because the repetition and insanity of it created a different desire. We now want peace. We look around and see everyone induced to petty fighting and are sickened. We see the desecration and indifference to life and it triggers our own past moral shortcomings. We are left tired and assaulted by the onslaught of triggers to keep humans in primal mode. It has become systemic.

If I could gift humans with one thing, it would be the ability to take them inside and offer calm like I do to my sweet Willy. Take them inside where there is rest from the insanity. Humans are so tired of the fighting. Their short memory and attention span has them forget the thousands of years of crusades they fought that is stored in their DNA. They forget all the times they were induced to war for the petty agenda of a larger than life character. They forget.

Instead of having the triggers of the anguishes of war prevail in them, only the triggers of the hate seem to be acerbated in them. It is like some intelligence knows exactly where to poke a needle in their brain and have them react in the most barbaric ways. It is like there was a campaign done to figure out the weak points in the human brain like they do to sell expensive cars. But this ad campaign induces people to hate. It is as if some people literally can't help themselves just like they have strong cravings and don't understand that they have a choice.

We all understand that agitation that crawls under the skin and prompts the barbaric behavior. We all understand the want and fear that ignites the body into reaction. We all understand the ridiculous beliefs that others have that seem like an affront to our own. But we also understand what it is to love.

If we can hold steady on the feeling of love. If we can resist the seductions of the primal urges. if we can realize that humanity itself is at stake and if we can get a sense that some outside source manipulating us like puppet, we can then find the fortitude to hold onto the simplicity of love and kindness so that it does not snuff out like a dying ember.

All that I write, all that I share and all that I offer to you through myself, is the beckoning to come inside from the barbarianism of the primal triggers and realize the potential you have as an aware being. The stakes must be pretty high to afford such an onslaught of negativity, We must be close to availing. Show love and kindness whenever you can. Put yourself in the other person's shoes. Find any commonality if you can. Perhaps do this exercise as well.

(Say each statement three times while tapping on your head and say it a fourth time while tapping on your chest.)

"I declare myself a surrogate for humanity in doing these taps"

"We release being trapped in primal mode; in all moments"

"We release being manipulated into primal mode; in all

moments"

"We release being enslaved to a reactionary state; in all moments"

"We release being affected by triggers that keep us in primal mode; in all moments"

"We eliminate the first cause in being in primal mode; in all moments"

"We remove all vivaxes between ourselves and primal mode; in all moments"

"We remove all tentacles between ourselves and primal mode; in all moments'

"We remove all programming and conditioning that primal mode has put on us; in all moments"

"We remove all engrams of primal mode; in all moments"

"We remove all masks, walls and armor that primal mode has put on us; in all moments"

"We send all energy matrices into the Light and Sound that induce us into or keep us in primal mode; in all moments"

"We command all complex energy matrices that induce us or keep us trapped in primal mode to be escorted into the Light and Sound; in all moments"

"We nullify all contracts with primal mode; in all moments"

"We dissipate all psychic streams of energy that support or perpetuate primal mode; in all moments"

"We withdraw all our energy from primal mode; in all moments"

"We release resonating or emanating with primal mode; in all moments"

"We transcend primal mode; in all moments"

"We shift our paradigm from primal mode to Universal Joy, Love, Abundance, Freedom, Health, Peace and Wholeness; in all moments"

"We are centered and empowered in Universal Joy, Love, Abundance, Freedom, Health, Peace and Wholeness; in all moments"

"We resonate, emanate, and are interconnected with all life in Universal Joy, Love, Abundance, Freedom, Health, Peace and Wholeness; in all moments"

Take a deep breath.

It may be difficult to do these. The resistance may seem incredible. You may think it is ridiculous. But I have watched them work. I have watched people's lives change from doing them. I have watched the world change for us doing them. So if you are feeling hopeless or ineffective as a human being, please add your intention to that of the angels and Guides by doing these taps. You may very well be the saving grace of humanity.

35: A DESECRATION TO THE ADVANCEMENT OF SOUL

It is simply impossible for so many diverse points of view to be developed and expressed in just one lifetime. If we only had one lifetime, there would be a much shallower approach to life. Because such intricate views, beliefs, preferences and styles take lifetimes to accumulate and to percolate underneath the surface of the human experience.

Those who believe in only one lifetime are the ones who are fixed in a certain vantage point. It is because they are stuck in the valley of what they have been given in raw materials in this one life. Petty vantage points breed petty views and petty lives. It is those who believe in one lifetime that are hell-bent on controlling the outcome of others as vital to their status in life.

They are the ones in "them versus us" mode. They are the ones that must preserve a purity of a race or borders to give them a sense of control. It is they who see differences in demographics, skin pigment and religions as non-negotiable differences between themselves and others. It is they who live in fear of death. It is they who seek control to make sense of such limited vantage points. It is they who are more easily induced to fear and who are self-righteous. They are the ones that stick their hands in other people's lives in the name of doing God's will.

But God's whole shtick is Love. It is power's shtick to control and judge.

Those of us who remember or merely realize we have past lives, feel a sense of familiarity in a stranger's stance. We have compassion for those who now wear the experiences that we once endured. We can peek over the threshold of all differences and see a glimmer of familiarity in a different state. We can tolerate what is different because we have been tolerating differences for what seems eternity.

It has lent those who understand that they have lived many lives a state of grace and a non-reactionary sense of being. It affords them more ability to relax in the expansiveness of the moment because they realize there is no hurry. All expiration dates looming in the future are made of illusion. We have all crossed over many times and know the procedure. We can relax more readily in the process of kicking off the physical body and continuing in the astral realm until we are called again to return to earth.

We also hold a conviction to improve the conditions on all of earth for we never know where we will land next time around. We are tired of the pettiness of war for we see clearly the power play behind each skirmish. We wish to see justice for the downtrodden because we have been the downtrodden, and it is a tiny victory for us each time the underdog wins. We see a familiarity in all faces and all bodies because we realize that we have been introduced to most souls we interact with in one lifetime or another. We have dwelt in similar circumstances and now have the luxury of viewing them from a different vantage point. We avoid putting labels on others because we remember being targeted for the labels that have been put on us in past times. In the past, labels have been a precursor to suffering. Most of all, we choose kindness first because we have an innate memory of when kindness was withheld from us and the memories of unkindness are too painful to be stoked.

If you are on the fence as to whether you have lived before, it may improve your advancement in awakening to delve into the questions.: What places do you want to visit? What cultures do you value? What periods in history seem interesting to you? What are you afraid of? What would you consider the worst way to die? It is good to remember that the things that we are afraid of are not things looming in our future but memories hidden in our past.

Resistance to believing in past lives many times is avoidance of all the loss and pain that has been buried there. But the losses and the pains also are the treasure map to where incredible love and adventure has been buried as well. Our greatest joy is seeing the recognition of familiarity in a stranger's eyes and meeting old loved ones again. Love at first sight is actually a joyous reunion between two familiar souls.

The belief in one life was actually adopted and precipitated at the beginning of the dark ages. It was then that high officials in the church would sell passageways to heaven to the rich and use fear of being damned to control others. This was taught in social studies class in grade school.

Even in the Bible, it was written that Jesus was a great soul who was coming back to earth as part of his mission. It was John the Baptist's role to announce the return of this great soul to earth. That was a scene in every depiction of the coming of Christ that was on television in the Seventies.

But the best reason for believing in past lives is because memories of our past slip through the screening process every day. It is where talents, beautiful memories and great adventures are stored. If one were to tap into such a treasure trove, they would discover their own depth, recognize their own greatness and develop compassion for themselves and self-worth. To deny one's self such personal and hard won memories is a great travesty to the human condition. It only serves fear and power to do such a thing. It is a desecration to the advancement of soul.

36: YOUR GIFT TO THE WORLD

I just woke up from a disturbing dream. It was about a Christmas party. Everyone was going to see the new baby. But the focus was all on the older sibling. There were no snacks, no gifts, no warmth and no joy in going to this event. Everyone was in their new clothes, but it didn't matter because nobody appreciated each other. Being all decked out in a setting where no one cared made everyone feel uncomfortable in their own skin. It is like they were always so unhappy but without any warmth around them, they felt it more.

The five year old was worshipped. Everything was about her. There was no place to really sit, but the child had the couch to stand on. She was singing songs out of a megaphone. They were cute, but it was mandated to adore them, and people were tired of it. The child was singing very loudly and was to be on television to sell her very expensive clothes. The proceeds would go to buying her more clothes.

At one point, I was going to play along and sing a song with her. But I had to stand on a lopsided stack of toys to emulate the child's height of standing on the back of the couch. I could not make a usable stool to stand on. A few of us went to the counter where the drinks were supposed to be served. It was laughable. There was just an empty counter next to an overflowing trash container of empty cups.

Everyone knew it was a joyless party and planned to leave to find somewhere they could go dancing. We made our excuses, and everyone was leaving early together. As we were leaving, one of the guests started mentioning the death of Lincoln and how it would be interesting to write a script around that. There was a bit of support for that as we left.

This dream had very deep meaning. The obnoxious toddler is what we have allowed the holiday to morph into. It was supposed to be honoring the birth of something sacred, but it has morphed into indulging the worst traits of our character that are taught and developed in our children. That is what we do when we indulge them to the degree that is happening. When we shamelessly spoil children in the name of all that is sacred, we do a disservice to all of humanity. This loveless party was what society has become. The baby never even made an appearance. It was all about the spoiled child accumulating more.

The lack of snacks and warmth was symbolic of there not being anything offered in a spiritual sense to anyone who attended the party. It was only an exercise in wearing new clothes with no joy or goodness imbued in the process. The void feeling in the guests is the byproduct of all the focus being on the child. There was none left for anyone else. Everyone was conditioned to go along with the joyless party and only secretly mocked the derided feeling of being obligated to attend. This depicts the lack of reverence in general.

Society has morphed into a demonstrative display of greed by using the baby (the birth of Christ) merely as an excuse to indulge. In the dream, trying to perform next to the child on a stool made of toys in order to bring some meaning back to the party was very important. It meant that no one is able to bring meaning back into society because of the limitations set up by outmoded belief systems. The toys represent limitations in beliefs, laws and doctrines that prevent anyone from gaining empowerment, awakening or transcending by totally following societal dictates.

The empty cups meant that all the sweetness and benefits that could possibly be accessed through the holiday have long been drunk by guests who had come and gone. The holiday has nothing to offer in sustenance except what people can possibly bring to it themselves. It has been overtaken long ago by materialism. Our society is totally depleted and devoid of being able to offer anything to its members except what the members bring to the table to share with others. All outlets of groups giving to the individuals have been bankrupt due to excessive materialism.

People leaving early is indicative of people showing up in society out of obligation but going somewhere else to express their spirituality. The woman wanting to write a script was showing how female energy is now being used in the attempt to freshen the old state of consciousness of society to prevent it from bleeding attendees. This is something to be aware of, and we are already seeing it transpire in the media by propping women up in male energy roles to seem like they are embracing female energy. Anything based on physical attributes and competition is male energy. The child in the dream was a pretty little girl. It depicted the short shelf life on physical attributes. Everyone else at the party was treated as irrelevant.

Here is your gift to the world. You can assist people everywhere in bowing out to worshipping materialism in the guise of paying homage to what is sacred.

(Say each statement a total of four times. The first three times say it while tapping continuously on the top of your head. Say it the fourth time while tapping on your chest.)

"We declare ourselves surrogates for humanity in doing these taps; in all moments."

"We release being manipulated by materialism; in all

moments."

"We release being deceived by materialism; in all moments."

"We release the genetic propensity to be materialistic; in all moments."

"We release being stuck in the primal mode of materialism; in all moments.

"We release being shackled to materialism; in all moments."

"We release allowing materialism to be our common denominator; in all moments."

"We release being subjugated by materialism; in all moments."

"We release being surrounded by materialism; in all moments."

"We release being indebted to materialism; in all moments."

"We nullify all contracts between ourselves and all materialism; in all moments."

"We convert all materialism back into Joy, Love, Abundance, Freedom, Health, Success, Truth and Wholeness; in all moments."

"We release all loyalty to materialism; in all moments."

"We remove all vivaxes between ourselves and all materialism; in all moments."

"We remove all tentacles between ourselves and all materialism; in all moments."

"We remove the claws of all materialism from our beingness; in all moments."

"We release being ruled by materialism; in all moments."

"We extract all materialism from our understanding of spirituality; in all moments."

"We remove all programming and conditioning that materialism has put on us; in all moments."

"We remove all engrams of materialism from our beingness; in all moments."

"We send all energy matrixes of materialism into the Light and Sound; in all moments."

"We command all complex energy matrixes of materialism to be escorted into the Light and Sound by our guides; in all moments."

"We send all energy matrixes into the Light and Sound that intrude upon our spiritualty; in all moments."

"We command all complex energy matrixes that intrude upon our spirituality to be escorted into the Light and

Sound by our guides; in all moments."

"We recant all vows and agreements between ourselves and materialism; in all moments."

"We strip all illusion off of materialism in all forms; in all moments."

"We remove all masks, walls, and armor from mass materialism; in all moments."

"We shatter all glass ceilings that materialism has put on us; in all moments."

"We eliminate the first cause in regard to materialism; in all moments."

"We remove all curses between ourselves and materialism; in all moments."

"We remove all blessings between ourselves and materialism; in all moments."

"We strip all entitlement off of all those immersed in materialism; in all moments."

"We remove all the pain, burden, and limitations that materialism has put on us; in all moments."

"We remove all the fear, futility and unworthiness that materialism has put on us; in all moments."

"We remove all the apathy, indifference, and devastation that materialism has put on us; in all

moments."

"We remove all the rejection, abandonment, and illusion of separateness that materialism has put on us; in all moments."

"We remove all that we have put on all others due to materialism; in all moments."

"We take back all that all materialism has taken from us; in all moments."

"We give back all that we have taken from others due to materialism; in all moments."

"We collapse and dissolve all materialism; in all moments."

"We release resonating or emanating with materialism; in all moments."

"We extract all materialism from our Sound Frequency; in all moments."

"We extract all materialism from our Light Emanation; in all moments."

"We extract all materialism from all 32 layers of our auric field; in all moments."

"We extract all materialism from our whole beingness; in all moments."

"We abolish all materialism as a construct; in all

moments."

"We shift our paradigm from all materialism to Joy, Love, Abundance, Freedom, Health, Success, Truth and Wholeness; in all moments."

"We transcend all materialism; in all moments."

"We are centered and empowered in Universal Joy, Love, Abundance, Freedom, Health, Success, Truth and Wholeness; in all moments."

"We resonate, emanate, and are interconnected with all life in Universal Joy, Love, Abundance, Freedom, Health, Success, Truth and Wholeness; in all moments."

What we do here is no small feat.

37: PREVENT A MANUFACTURED WAR

There is no need to subscribe to fear and conjecture. We are better than that. In fact, the more that we maintain our center, the less it feeds ignoble intentions like perpetuating and marinating a manufactured war. These taps are very effective. May doing them bring you incredible relief in knowing that WE THE PEOPLE are too savvy to sit by and be manipulated by such a tactic because we are savvy enough now to realize that it has always been the blood, sweat and fervor of individuals that have been milked to maintain the ugly beast. Here is to us starving out the ugliest beast and emaciating power and control in the world.

(Say each statement three times while tapping on your head and say it a fourth time while tapping on your chest. Then go on to the next.)

"I declare myself a surrogate for humanity in doing these taps; in all moments."

"We strip all denial off of the world in believing that war is manufactured; in all moments."

"We release allowing a manufactured war to drive humanity; in all moments."

"We dissipate the systemic indifference that allows a manufactured war to limit the quality of life for all; in all moments."

"We remove all masks, walls, and armor off of manufactured war; in all moments."

"We remove all masks, walls, and armor off of those using a manufactured war to deceive the populace; in all moments."

"We release allowing a manufactured war to strip individuals of civil liberties; in all moments."

"We release allowing a manufactured war to strip individuals of their ability to discern; in all moments."

"We prevent all individuals from engaging in a manufactured war; in all moments."

"We prevent a manufactured war from pimping us out for the gain of big business; in all moments."

"We prevent a manufactured war from perpetuating oligarchies; in all moments."

"We prevent a manufactured war hiding the transgressions of their deceit; in all moments."

"We release allowing a manufactured war to diminish

our freedom; in all moments."

"We release passively watching while big business or oligarchies manufacture war; in all moments."

"We strip all illusion off of a manufactured war; in all moments."

"We release being duped into giving our passion to a manufactured war; in all moments."

"We release being separated from our humanity by a manufactured war; in all moments."

"We release being manipulated by a manufactured war; in all moments."

"We release deferring to a manufactured war in all things sacred; in all moments."

"We release allowing a manufactured war to frame our perception of reality; in all moments."

"We release allowing a manufactured war to shove an agenda down our throat; in all moments."

"We break up power brokers that use a manufactured war to enslave humanity; in all moments."

"We release being kept in ignorance to a manufactured war; in all moments."

"We release being duped by a manufactured war; in all moments."

"We release being entertained by a manufactured war; in all moments."

"We release engaging a manufactured war; in all moments."

"We release being stripped of our progressiveness by a manufactured war; in all moments."

"We release being complacent with the manipulative ploys of a manufactured war; in all moments."

"We release having our humanity gutted by a manufactured war; in all moments."

"We release being pimped into a manufactured war; in all moments."

"We eliminate the first cause in the creation of a manufactured war; in all moments."

"We release being immersed in a manufactured war; in all moments."

"We strip all illusion and defenses off those who use a manufactured war to gain or profit; in all moments."

"We release converting our sacred devotion to God into deference to a manufactured war; in all moments."

"We release being enslaved to a manufactured war; in all moments."

"We release diminishing ourselves by allowing a

manufactured war to hold our attention; in all moments."

"We remove all vivaxes between ourselves and a manufactured war; in all moments."

"We remove all tentacles between ourselves and a manufactured war; in all moments."

"We withdraw all our energy from a manufactured war; in all moments."

"We release having blind faith in a manufactured war; in all moments."

"We collapse and dissolve all manufactured wars; in all moments."

"We remove all programming and conditioning that manufactured wars have put on us; in all moments."

"We remove all individual and universal engrams of a manufactured war; in all moments."

"We release allowing a manufactured war to induce us to fear or hatred; in all moments."

"We release allowing a manufactured war to rob us of our voice or dignity; in all moments."

"We release the belief that a manufactured war is inevitable; in all moments."

"We send all energy matrices into the light and sound

that enable a manufactured war to happen; in all moments."

"We command all complex energy matrices that enable a manufactured war to happen be escorted into the light and sound; in all moments."

"We send all energy matrices into the light and sound that blind us to the deceit of creating a manufactured war; in all moments."

"We command all complex energy matrices that blind us to the deceit of creating a manufactured war to be escorted into the light and sound; in all moments."

"We send all energy matrices into the light and sound that perpetuate a manufactured war; in all moments."

"We command all complex energy matrices that perpetuate a manufactured war to be escorted into the light and sound; in all moments."

"We release being deceived by the makings of a manufactured war; in all moments."

"We recant all vows and agreements between ourselves and manufactured wars; in all moments."

"We remove all curses between ourselves and manufactured wars; in all moments."

"We remove all blessings between ourselves and manufactured wars; in all moments."

"We remove all payoffs to all those who manufactured war to profit, wield power or peddle an ignoble agenda; in all moments."

"We sever all strings, cords and psychic connection between ourselves and a manufactured war; in all moments."

"We dissipate all psychic streams of energy that allow a manufactured war to go unchecked; in all moments."

"We dissolve all karmic ties between ourselves and a manufactured war; in all moments."

"We remove all the pain, burden, limitations, fear, futility, unworthiness and illusion of separateness that a manufactured war has put on us; in all moments."

"We bury all those who manufacture war in the weight of their own ignoble intentions; in all moments."

"We remove all muscle memory that causes us to defer to a manufactured war; in all moments."

"We break all energy grids between ourselves and a manufactured war; in all moments."

"We take back all the joy, love, abundance, freedom, health, success, security, companionship, creativity, peace, life, wholeness, beauty, enthusiasm contentment, spirituality, enlightenment, confidence, ability to discern, and empowerment that a manufactured war has taken from us; in all moments."

"We disarm the ability of a manufactured war to desecrate earth; in all moments."

"We disarm the ability of a manufactured war to separate us from our humanity; in all moments."

"We strip manufactured war of its illusion of propriety; in all moments."

"We strip manufactured war of its illusion of noble intention; in all moments."

"We disarm manufactured war from the ability to dwindle our life, liberties and pursuit of happiness; in all moments."

"We crumble and dissolve all constructs created by a manufactured war; in all moments."

"We nullify all contracts with manufactured war; in all moments."

"We strip all illusion off those who benefit from using a manufactured war to wield power or gain wealth; in all moments."

"We eliminate the first cause in all mandates of a manufactured war; in all moments."

"We hold open a portal for Universal peace in all; in all moments."

"We release confusing manufactured war with a noble intention; in all moments."

"We release confusing a manufactured war with necessity; in all moments."

"We release resonating or emanating with a manufactured war; in all moments."

"We extract all of manufactured war from our individual and Universal Sound Frequency; in all moments."

"We extract all of manufactured war from our individual and Universal Light Emanation; in all moments."

"We extract all of manufactured war from all 32 layers of our individual and Universal aura; in all moments."

"We extract all of manufactured war from our whole beingness; in all moments."

"We shift our paradigm from manufactured war to individual and Universal Joy, Love, Abundance, Freedom Health, Peace, Strength, Empowerment and Integrity; in all moments."

"We transcend manufactured war; in all moments."

"We are centered and empowered in Universal Peace; in all moments."

"We infuse Universal Peace into our Sound frequency; in all moments."

"We imbue Universal Peace into our Light emanation; in all moments."

"We resonate, emanate and are interconnected to all life in Universal Peace; in all moments."

38: REGAINING SPIRITUAL PERSPECTIVE

Besides publishing nine books to help people and simply surviving to get my message of individual empowerment out, facilitating my first retreat is the major accomplishment of my life. It was profound how easily the days flowed without over-planning talks and the agenda.

The Guides who prompt me to do all this insisted that nobody come prepared with what they were going to say before the event. They explained that when you write an outline for an event, you are creating the structure for it and then fitting people in almost like an afterthought. With the events I facilitate, I wait to see who attends and *then* speak to their specific needs and issues. Doing this made for a very profound event.

There were my favorite parts of the event. Seeing everyone who was already scheduled to attend show up at the book signing was marvelous. It wasn't about the books. It was everyone coming together and getting to know each other before the event started. It was amazing how everyone from different backgrounds came together as if they knew each other. They actually did in a way. We have all been together for many lifetimes. So the book signing was a way to get reacquainted.

I also gave this impromptu gift to those staying in the hotel. I offered to go to each one of their rooms after the book signing and do a clearing of the energy in it, so they could be more comfortable resting. It was a way of energetically tucking them in. We went to each room as a group. Everyone got to observe the clearing that was done in each room. Then we left that person off at their room and did this until everyone was delivered lovingly to their destination.

It seemed to help because some people had experiences of great peace in this clarity of space. Two people who were sharing the room--both individually and together--experienced a huge energetic tree of life in their room. They were amazed that the other could see what they were seeing with their eyes. It was a loving presence of serenity and protection.

During this pilgrimage to all the rooms, there was a member of the hotel staff who was transporting luggage. I was prompted to ask him if I could release an issue from his heart. He allowed it. I told him what it referenced. It was a personal struggle in family dynamics that he couldn't even speak about to others. He looked surprised but grateful for the gift.

When attendees used the shuttle, they were transported by this young man and were surprised that he was so receptive to me being in the hotel. They were expecting to feel awkward about explaining why they would be staying at the hotel. Instead, the man seemed excited for them. I got to speak to him the next day and he explained how he was struggling to get his credits accredited to him that he needed for a degree. But the next morning after I helped him, he was told he actually had enough credits for his degree and some to put towards a second degree.

The morning of the first day of the retreat, I really didn't know what to expect from everyone. I know what I do, but I had never been able to command a room and work on a whole group of people at once. Everyone sat in tables that formed a horseshoe shape around the center. I could speak to the group all at once and each individual as necessary. Some who attended had never even heard of me until a friend mentioned the retreat. Then they knew they "needed" to be there. They were not disappointed.

I went around the horseshoe tables and did a general clearing on everyone. But then I went up to each person and gave them a SFT tap (Spiritual Freedom Technique) to do specifically for themselves. Everyone else in the room did them as well, but the person knew it was their deep issue being pulled out like a little embedded tangle of hair.

I would see the person brace against the truth they were about to receive. It may have been painful initially for them. But it was more painful expecting the worst to be uncovered. There was no worst. There was only the nugget that needed to be released with no blame, judgment or scolding. It was beautifully scripted by the Gods. Everyone could actually see the other attendees soften through the two days.

They dropped so many of their personal defenses, grudges, justifications, excuses, and reasons for not shining in their empowerment. Without the nugget issue, there was nothing to justify. It was like removing energetic corns from the people's energy systems-- things that have caused them so much pain and discomfort in compensating for them. Then the attendees lightened up realizing that they were just gone.

In the next section, I put my massage table in the middle of the room and worked on people individually. Part of me thought this would be tedious for people to watch. But I was supposed to demonstrate the physiology of healing. Think of it as doing faith healing in slow time so everyone can understand the process. It would be similar to a magician going through his tricks to strip all the illusion off of them. The magic is taken out of healing, and it is exposed as the powerful physiological process that it is. Maybe this hasn't been done because healers who do spontaneous healing don't know the process. Perhaps breaking it down for the world so they can accept natural healing is my forte.

I worked on someone who was having issues with her thyroid. Apparently, no medicines were working. After her demonstration, everyone could understand why. The emotional issue being stored in her thyroid was that of being a little girl and watching her mother being murdered in front of her eyes. It dried up her security and innocence in that lifetime. It was bleeding through to this one. The more she got connected to her innate innocence through her spiritual endeavor, the more this trauma from a past life was unnerved and creating an issue in her present life.

I experienced that trauma for her as she lay on the table and led her through some taps to release that pain that was trapped in her energy field and rooted to the thyroid. It is almost like burping her energy field of the trauma. As she lay on the table, I led her through such taps as, "I release watching momma be killed in all moments," and "I release having momma being taken from me in all moments." As I am enthralled in helping her release this important issue, I am slightly concerned that others in the room may get bored if I spend my time on one person. When I looked up and around, there was not a dry eye in the room. Great! Everyone released this primal issue. Everyone benefited from this process.

Another thing I was instructed to do by the Guides was to download all that I do as a healer into the brains of everyone attending. They explained to me that two energy systems can exchange information as easily as two cell phones can. So they instructed me to go around the room and gift everyone in attendance with the awareness and ability to do what I do. This is very important because I am not here to be singled out as a dynamic healer. I am here to teach the skills and retrain the individual to remember how to do the things we were all once taught to do outwardly. These abilities were stripped away lifetime by lifetime as a means of control. But now, to advance humanity, it is important that all individuals remember how to be empowered and take off the unworthiness, victim and complaining shackles.

This was some of the attendees' favorite part. Some got dizzy after it. One attendee could see trees undulate the way I see them. Some just felt a sense of wellbeing. One dynamic healer was crying because she knew that this is what she had been asking for many lifetimes. It was funny for me because I have been hidden in plain sight by the Guides as a means of survival during a dark time. But now I am being seen and all the attendees recognized the great gift they had been given merely for accepting the source. I was not invisible to them as the dynamic healer I am. The veil had been lifted.

It was also magical for me to listen to the friendships

and connections being formed around me. People who met just a day ago were transformed into dear ones by the experience of the retreat. If this could be done in a small group, imagine what would happen if more and more people had the experience that the attendees did. The love and connection were something I had only felt a while ago in a group. But that inexplicable feeling of love for all life was replaced by personality worship and an agenda as they grew. We had tapped into the secret source of divinity on earth. Everyone attending felt it.

After facilitating this retreat, I thought I would get time to rest. It is true I am still processing the incredible vibration that the retreat brought to the planet. But the very next day, I got instructions about the next retreat. It was very specific in some ways.

The Guides want me to create the vibration of world peace in the next retreat. The vision that most people have of world peace is that it is a welfare state where nobody works. This is the lie that has been perpetuated. The lie that has been perpetrated amongst some of the truest seekers in the world is that world peace is not possible. This has left many gifted spiritual people in a state of apathy. They have been left thinking that they have to wait to get out of the body to experience this. That is a male energy perspective. Female energy radiates peace, joy, and love from wherever her center is even, and especially, if that is on earth.

One of the greatest spiritually adept people in the last century was Paul Twitchell. He had put the premise out to the world that world peace was impossible. He was remarkably accurate in his work but also was a wordsmith, like myself. It is true that there is no world peace in the Third Dimension. And so what he stated was accurate from that vantage point. But we are now in the Fifth Dimension, and it is time to awaken to world peace. It seems like there was a reason he emphatically put that statement out there. He knows how power corrupts. He was saying that there was no world peace to throw the power mongers of the time off the scent of figuring a way to harvest it to their own will.

Paul Twitchell knew of me. He mentioned Madame Blavatsky in his early writings. He knew I was incarnated, and he was throwing the scent of world peace anywhere away from me so that I could stay protected through the harsh conditioning I had to endure. There were times when it wasn't certain I would survive the training of this life. But I did. Even the diminishing stance he may have taken on females not being spiritual equals to males was a way to throw power mongers off the scent. I may not have survived without him doing this.

There was one more memory from the retreat that was very profound to me. During the afternoon session of the second day, we all did a set of taps as a surrogate for humanity. It was to bring everyone out of the enslavement of linear existence and into exponential existence. Afterwards, we all went to lunch at a salad place. There was an amazing stream of bright sunlight shining into the window and everyone was joyous. Then I felt the joy of the Ancient Ones on the other side of the veil. They were celebrating as well. What they had come here to do was finally being done. The seeds of World Peace were planted.

That is why at the last retreat, all the attendees were welcome to bring their gifts and share them with the other attendees for a small portion of the event. The chaos, self-worth and accomplishment create a beautiful vibration similar to world peace.

We expound the joyous activity and create the ripple of world peace by everyone sharing their gifts, and send it out to the whole planet to embrace. That is what has been missing from the world. Along with female empowerment, the vibrations of world peace are returning to the planet to bring an incredible shift in consciousness. That is what my facilitated retreats entail. I would love to see you at the next one. Spaces are limited so if you are feeling a calling, please sign up early.

39: TAKING CLASSES IN THE DREAM STATE

Last night, in the more subtle realms, I attended classes. When others dream, they may seem disjointed or make no sense. But the more you practice conscious dreaming, the more the distortions fall away and your dream life becomes an extension of your waking life.

It seemed like the class was a refresher course for me. I was there merely to encourage the other attendees. They were people from all over the world. The classrooms were more of a warehouse of creativity with artwork and individuality brimming over. The warehouse felt like a co-op for adults of all walks of life. They were learning many lessons. I wasn't certain what until I reflected on the classes.

It seems that the people were very comfortable coming together. It was the feeling that you may get in fulfilling a "program" that you were ordered to attend by the state. The people were there begrudgingly at first, but then they got used to being in the class and were actually starting to let down their guards and participate unabashedly. They enjoyed that I was there and wanted me to participate as well.

There was a special event this night. It gave me an understanding I was to take back to this state. It was an understanding of what I was actually attending. It was a mockup of an open market. Its purpose was to give people experiences that they had not yet had in their physical life. There was a vendor there from the Middle East. Perhaps many people have fears of the Middle East so he was assisting in helping them overcome them. He was giving his wares away as examples. He gave me a dish of exotic meats to eat. They were leathery and chewy. He also had vegetable as well, but I did not receive any of those. The lesson was tailored just for me. Because I have been starved in this life, food is very important to me. He was using what people love, to overcome what they fear. That is how it is done. He is obviously an Ancient One or Spirit Guide.

The meat was not appealing to me but that was the whole point, to experience things that would not be agreeable usually and to accept them. He told me that food in his country was very scarce and what I was eating was considered a luxury. He showed me his vegetable dishes and said that in his country they were more valuable than gold. That is how rare they are. It was a means of putting the gluttony that Americans have in perspective. He was balancing out imbalances of all kind with his subtle presentation. That is also how it works.

I then realized what I was witnessing in the class. I was witnessing people, who were set in their ways, taking mandatory classes in the dream state to be more flexible and to get a sense of what others on earth had to deal with. The classes that were being held were classes on compassion. There are so many people on earth who still need to experience so much of what others go through to develop compassion. We need all individuals to have compassion for humanity to transcend to a higher vibratory rate. It is tedious for some of us who already have love and compassion for all life. These classes were assisting with an upgrade.

The classes that I witnessed in the dream state were people who struggle with relating to the plight of others, to have the experiences needed to get over fears and to be more aware and compassionate. At this point, their attendance is mandatory. We are all getting to the point of needing to recognize our connection with all other beings. These classes were ways to bring everyone to the table, in a sense, of kindness, forgiveness, sincerity, integrity, and honesty. I am so grateful and relieved to know these classes are taking place in the more subtle realms. I am happy to think of some of the most stubborn people being mandated to attend. The warehouse was full of classrooms and classes.

As I am writing this now, I realize that the Exponential

Empowerment Expo that I have been told to facilitate by my Guides is a reflection of these classes here on earth. They are a means of seeding the earth with universal peace and compassion. May all who are being drawn to attend find a means of attending. They are a means of bringing more of the subtle realms to earth and to help all of humanity awaken.

ABOUT THE AUTHOR

Jen Ward, LMT, is a Reiki Master, Shaman, medical intuitive, gifted healer, and an innovator of healing practices. She is at the leading edge of energy work providing an upgrade of understanding of healing from the Third Dimension to the Fifth. She takes the mystery out of what is called faith healing by explaining the physiology behind it in common language. Faith healing is not magic or super powers but merely a heart centered intention manifesting its capabilities. Jen says that there is nothing that a pure intention fueled by a loving heart cannot accomplish. Humans are so conditioned to come from their mind and this creates the limitations on their abilities. The heart has no limits. Jen explains in the Fifth Dimension, we are all whole but we have brought with us our engrams (ingrained conditioning) from the Third Dimension. It is relatively easy for people to release their issues because in the Fifth Dimension, they are already whole. The work that Jen does is in empowering the individual to realize what they are truly capable of.

Jen is considered a sangoma, a traditional African Shaman, who channels ancestors, emoting sounds and vocalizations in ceremonies. An interesting prerequisite to being a sangoma is to have survived the brink of death. When Jen was first approached with the knowledge of being a sangoma, she had not yet fulfilled this prerequisite. However, in April 2008, when she came back to society on the brink of starvation as a result of traumatic involuntary imprisonment, the qualification had been met. She returned to the world of humanity a devout soul inspired to serve.

Her special abilities have also allowed her to innovate a revolutionary technique for finding lost pets by performing an emotional release on the animal. Using this method, she has successfully reunited many lost pets with their owners.

Jen currently works as a long-distance emotional release facilitator, public speaker, and consultant. Her special modality encompasses a holistic overview of her clients from all vantage points, including their physical, emotional, causal, and mental areas, ultimately benefiting their work, home, family, and especially spiritual lives.

You can find Jen here:
www.jenuinehealing.com/
Twitter: @jenuinehealing
Facebook: Facebook.com/JenuineHealingwithJenWard/

OTHER BOOKS BY JEN WARD

Enlightenment Unveiled: *Expound into Empowerment.* This book contains case studies to help you peel away the layers to your own empowerment using the tapping technique.

Grow Where You Are Planted: *Quotes for an Enlightened "Jeneration."* Inspirational quotes that are seeds to shift your consciousness into greater awareness.

Perpetual Calendar: *Daily Exercises to Maintain Balance and Harmony in Your Health, Relationships and the Entire World.* 369 days of powerful taps to use as a daily grounding practice for those who find meditation difficult.

Children of the Universe. Passionate prose to lead the reader lovingly into expanded consciousness.

Letters of Accord: *Assigning Words to Unspoken Truth.* Truths that the Ancient Ones want you to know to redirect your life and humanity back into empowerment.

The Do What You Love Diet: *Finally, Finally, Finally Feel Good in Your Own Skin.* Revolutionary approach to regaining fitness by tackling primal imbalances in relationship to food.

Emerging From the Mist: *Awakening the Balance of Female Empowerment in the World.* Release all the issues that prevent someone from embracing their female empowerment.

Affinity for All Life: *Valuing Your Relationship with All Species.* This book is a means to strengthen and affirm your relationship with the animal kingdom.

The Wisdom of the Trees. If one is struggling for purpose, they can find love, and truth by tuning into the *Wisdom of the Trees*.

www.ingramcontent.com/pod-product-compliance
Lightning Source LLC
Chambersburg PA
CBHW071655090426
42738CB00009B/1536